HE ...

Personal journey ... healing through Guillain-Barré syndrome.

Soli Deo Gloria
Glory to God Alone

*They triumphed over him by the blood of the Lamb and by
the word of their testimony; they did not love their lives so
much as to shrink from death.*
Revelation 12:11 (NIV)

*A few names in this book have been changed for privacy
purposes. Names of my direct family members, most friends,
and the hospital visitor named Angel remain original.*

Cover illustrations by Sara Frisina.

Interior formatting design by Keyminor Publishing (more information can be found on FaceBook @KeyminorPublishing).

ACKNOWLEDGMENTS

First and foremost, thank you to Jesus Christ my Lord, Savior, and Healer. *Matthew 19:26 (NIV)*, Jesus looked at them and said, "With man this is impossible, but with God all things are possible."

Second, thank you to my mom and dad for always being there for me no matter what. You have always pointed me back to the Lord. To my husband, Wayne, for sticking by me as a constant friend before we were married, an amazing partner while married, and for loving me just the way I am. Thank you to my kids for loving me always and forgiving me for all of my mom mistakes.

To my family, friends, doctors, nurses, hospital staff, and even the strangers that held my family and me while I journeyed through Guillain-Barré, thank you. Each and every one of you is stored in my heart.

Ashley Soden, thank you for chasing me down and insisting I start writing. I struggled to begin, and you are one of the reasons I finally embarked on these pages. Thank you, Kirsten Oliphant, my friend and fellow author, for all of your advice in this self-publishing journey. Thank you Diana Wilson for taking the time out of your busy schedule to snap some recent pictures for me. You are a gem! Thank you, Penning and Planning, Judy's Proofreading, Keyminor Publishing, Sara Frisina, and all the professionals that edited, proofread, formatted, and cover created to make the finished product shine. Thank you to my wonderful Healing Prayer Ministry, Prophetic Prayer Ministry, and Prayer Team Ministry partners that kept affirming God's plan in this book. You spoke the confirmation words over me and put me back on track each time I lost my way in the writing process.

Each and every one of you has greatly impacted my life.

INTRODUCTION

In order to fully appreciate the healing that takes place within these pages, you must first understand the lasting devastation that many Guillain-Barré syndrome patients endure.

Guillain-Barré syndrome (GBS) is a very sudden onset of symptoms that occur approximately thirty days after an illness, surgery, immunization, infection or other "trigger" that causes a person's body to go into a seemingly natural immune response to fight off the "invader." After fighting off said "intruder," the body's immune system says, "Wait, there is more to kill, we must continue to attack!" Thus the body's own immune system begins to attack its own nervous system, stripping it of the very important insulation-like myelin sheathing.

The nervous system controls everything from motor skills, speech, sight, pain, sensations, and natural organ function. When the nervous system is stripped, in various stages and places of the body, it can lead to weakness, numbness, tingling, extreme pain, phantom sensations, paralysis, blindness, arthritis, multiple vision, loss of voice, starvation, chronic fatigue, organs shutting down, and even death. It is like being locked inside a body that won't respond to the simplest of tasks while the mind continues to work perfectly.

Most patients are left with residual symptoms long after they "recover," spending a lifetime grasping at straws with treatments and pain medications, using wheelchairs, walkers, canes, leg braces, and other means to simply get through the day. Long-term and lifelong tingling, pain, arthritis, and chronic fatigue are frequent effects. Less common are those patients who are left completely paralyzed, intubated and bedridden, just so they can cling to the last vestiges of hope for life.

This memoir is my journey of the childhood years that prepared me to not only endure GBS, but to also push forward to "fly" on the new wings God had given me through being completely and miraculously healed.

The first part of my healing had to be "walked out daily," and the last part of my healing was sudden and complete. So, come along with me and gain hope. My prayer is that all who read this book will be utterly and wholly healed.

FLASH FORWARD

BLIND

For we walk by faith, not by sight.

2 CORINTHIANS 5:7

I kicked my parents out of my hospital room. Not out of anger, but out of love. They had been taking turns curling up in the little green vinyl ICU hospital chair by my bed, only to wake up more exhausted the next day than they had been the night before. I knew they would go crazy with sleep deprivation, so I made them go home and ordered them to not return until they had slept, showered, and eaten. I assured them I would be fine; after all, the nurses checked on me all night long. And if I died...that was okay too. No, I didn't tell them it was okay if I died that night—

they wouldn't have left if I did—but, seriously, after everything I had been through, I was so ready to go home; to Heaven. Little did I know that THAT night would be one of the worst, and one of the best, nights of my illness. God met me in my room that night.

Sleep eludes those in extreme pain. It comes in short spurts, more like passing out and coming to. This night I actually slept and the nurses did not wake me up. They came by my room throughout the night to take my blood, measure my lung capacity, do a chest X-ray, but when they saw that I was actually sleeping, they had mercy on me and let me rest.

It was relatively quiet for an ICU, which is always bustling with activity, tests and emergencies. When I finally did startle awake in the middle of the night, as I so often did, I immediately knew that this time something was different. An ICU is never dark. There are always bright lights in the hall, casting their glow around the window blinds, and dim lights in the patients' rooms. The machines cast strange blinking lights on the walls and ceiling, along with the beeping and whirring sounds that inform anyone within range that they are doing their jobs.

Shadows ink across the ceiling without invitation, and shoes squeak on the floor in the hallway outside as the nurses make their rounds. A nightlight is never necessary in the ICU. But this night, when I opened my eyes during the wee hours of darkness, I realized that something was off. Something was wrong. Yes, everything was wrong; I was dying after all. My organs and body were shutting down on me, paralyzed and unable to make my limbs respond to the easiest of tasks, but this was different; this was worse. I heard the beeping of my machines and looked in their direction. Nothing. I glanced toward the window where I knew the bright lights from the nurses' station glared incessantly, even when I was trying to sleep. Nothing. I scoured the expanse before me, yet not a glimmer of light pierced my eyes. I could not see. I was blind.

This time my limbs did what I asked. Just as my mind willed it, my hand reached out into the darkness to grasp... what? I'm not sure what I was reaching for. My heart was calling out to Jesus and my body responded by stretching out my hand and arm into the air before me. But then the unexpected happened. Something, someone, grasped my hand and held on tight. An angelic Latin voice spoke to me in a deep slow rhythm, that sounded like a rich gentle lullaby, that could rock me into a sweet and endless sleep. "Hello, Natalie, my name is Angel and I have come to pray with you."

My breath gasped out of me in pure anguish when I realized I was not alone. Somehow, I was able to eek out the words, "I'm blind. I can't see." Tears began to stream down my face in silent tracks of pain. No sobs broke forth from my chest, but my tears told the truth of my deep distress better than any feeble words ever could.

We connected in that moment, Angel and I. His pure love poured over me and I knew—KNEW—that I was not alone. Yes, I knew that God was always with me, but this timing, this voice, this personal lullaby that was so tender and full of compassion told me that GOD WAS WITH ME, even at my very lowest of lows.

I had always feared blindness. Even as a child I knew that I never wanted to go blind. The thought of navigating this world in darkness was scary. Even with that trace of apprehension living inside of me, I never gave blindness more than a passing thought. I didn't think loss of sight was anything I would personally experience. Even with everything going wrong with my body due to Guillain-Barré, I never expected to open my eyes to complete darkness, being swallowed by a void so black it seemed to press against me on every side. This darkness was thick and heavy, like a weighted blanket trying to smother out my very existence.

Angel prayed for me. His voice was like a musical ballad written just for me, nourishing and fixing a deep part of my soul that had withered. His prayer of worship was a weapon that broke the back of fear and allowed a warrior to rise up in its place. In the dark of night and blindness, he prayed and gripped my hand like an anchor, steadying me for the remainder of my fight ahead. His prayers tickled my ears while my tears ran in rivulets, soaking the pillow under my head.

After a long and gentle silence, Angel released my hand and tucked me in. I rolled over with a renewed sense of hope and a peace that passes all understanding. I fell into a gentle sleep and awoke the next morning able to see again.

Fear had been vanquished, and my master's hands had touched both my eyes and my heart. I could see the light of day again.

ONE

A BUTTERFLY?

*So then, just as you received Christ Jesus as Lord,
continue to live your lives in him, rooted and built
up in him, strengthened in the faith as you were
taught, and overflowing with thankfulness.*

COLOSSIANS 2:6-7
(NIV)

Even though I lived it, I am not exactly sure how to put
my journey into words. How does a person begin a
story that is bigger than themselves, something so intense
that they now define events along the timeline of their life
as pre-event or post-event? God was in the minute details of
this story I lived, so it is difficult to capture the despair, joy,
fear, awe, insanity, loneliness, miracle, and wonder of it all.

Take a butterfly, for instance. How could she accurately
tell her insect friends that she was once an entirely different
creature, yet still the very same insect as always, only now
she can fly?

Would they believe that her younger years were spent crawling—without wings—and munching on herbs, not sipping nectar? Would they believe her when she told them that she had to shed her very skin several times just so she could grow? Could they fathom the experience of the cocoon—its isolation, its loneliness and its darkness? Would they believe the physical and mental transformation that takes place in such a strangled and confined space? What about the struggle of escape—how can the butterfly even put that into accurate words? Now that she has wings, she talks about her past memories as pre-cocoon or post-cocoon; pre-wings or post-wings. Her friends may wonder why she always defines events in her life that way because they don't understand how altering that event was to her.

No, unless you are the caterpillar that became a butterfly, the one that went from crawling to flying, you cannot fully fathom the depths of pain or the joy of flight, but you can catch a glimpse of the wonder of the metamorphosis, the miracle of God's creation, if you simply sit, watch, and listen. Well, here is my story, if you dare to read it, of how I became that butterfly.

My life was enchanted, as far as I was concerned. I cherished everything about my life. I had a father and a mother who loved me, a close-knit family full of cousins, a doting grandmother, and at least one best friend at a time. Joy simply bubbled inside me. As a stranger looking into my life from the outside, you probably wouldn't have known that I was so joyful. You would simply have labeled me as quiet, shy, sheltered, stoic or some other "introvert" description. I did not react much to good or bad things. To others it seemed that the outside world had no effect on me. But inside...I noticed everything.

Nothing slipped by my all-seeing eyes, my discerning

ears, and my sensitive spirit. I soaked it all in, the sights, sounds, and thoughts. World events weighed heavy on my heart and mind, and family events weighed even heavier, both the good and the bad. I savored each and every experience around me and stored it up for later use, hoping to skip some of those noticed failures and mimic the successes. That quiet, seemingly unaffected, girl was a storehouse of emotional and informational files. I simply leaned on the Lord for all the tough stuff and peacefully enjoyed the good.

My mind seemed to never shut down. I was a deep thinker; often lying on the green grass watching clouds float by or staring at an hourglass as the sand slipped away, while pondering the depths of the vast and untapped universe, the intricacies of the Bible, and unfathomable character of God. My spirit was constantly praying, so much so that I would often wake up from sleep in the night to find myself praying or singing out loud, with tears wetting my cheeks.

I appreciated talking to God as if He were sitting right next to me, us the very best of friends. I asked Him questions and sat quietly awaiting answers. I praised Him and simply reveled in His presence.

This may sound strange to you for a little girl to act this way, but it is true...that is who I was, and still am to a large degree. Don't get me wrong, I was still a kid. Messy. Loud. Disobedient. Ever learning. I said hurtful things to people I loved and was more often than not thought of as rude because of how direct and unfiltered my mouth spoke. My actions did not always reflect my love for the Lord, or the people around me. I couldn't keep my room clean to save my life and I was frequently caught daydreaming during school. Just like any kid, I had my good moments and my faults, but I also had a very simple faith in my creator, Jesus. If the Bible said it, I believed it. Period!

More than that simple faith or belief, I had God experiences. His fingerprints are all over my life. I smelled Him, saw Him, and felt Him, over and over again. I will share some of those experiences with you as we journey together, for they not only let you see into who I was before I became ill, but they also tell the story of our daddy God so well. I do believe that no earthly book can accurately contain how big God is, or how big He has been in my life (or your life if you let Him), but I hope this book will give you just a glimpse.

TWO

THE CATERPILLAR YEARS

*And why do you worry about clothes? See how the
flowers of the field grow. They do not labor or spin.
Yet I tell you that not even Solomon in all his
splendor was dressed like one of these. If that is how
God clothes the grass of the field, which is here today
and tomorrow is thrown into the fire, will he not
much more clothe you—you of little faith?*

MATTHEW 6:28-30
(NIV)

Have you ever watched a young caterpillar grow? It
has lifecycles. Starting at its very smallest size, it eats
and eats and eats until it sheds its skin and doubles in size.
Then it does this again. And again. And again. Until it is
rather huge for a caterpillar. Much bigger than its future,
yet still unfathomable, butterfly body that is more wing than
torso. Why is that?

I went through much of that same cycle growing up.

Not so much in a physical sense—I am 5' 3" fully grown, so I was always a small person—but very much in the spiritual-growth and faith-building way. I always thought God was teaching me and preparing me for my life and ministry as an adult, and He was, but I had no idea how much I was going to need the strong foundation of my young caterpillar growing years in order to press through the most challenging physical battle of my life as a young adult.

At the age of six, my first skin-shedding event took place. Of course, I had already been "eating" by quietly observing everything around me, which is part of why I noticed the change that happened in my home.

Up until this point in my life, everything was great, as far as I knew. My parents were loving and engaged in my life. I didn't know hardship, and I was a typical kid. My parents were wonderful. I never heard them fighting, cursing, drinking or doing anything that would send signals to a kid that something had changed in them or their lives. But something did change: my parents found God. Or, really, God transformed my parents. They "got saved."

There was a very noticeable shift in the atmosphere of our home, at least to me, the quiet observer. Nothing egregious had been happening, so nothing egregious stopped happening to signal "big change ahead, left lane ends, move to the right." I simply noticed peace in our home. An undercurrent of tranquility that I never knew had been missing prior to my parents inviting Jesus to be their Lord and Savior. The difference was so immediate and intense, especially in my dad's—Wayman's—demeanor, a man who went from agnostic to Christian in one fell swoop, that it prompted my six-year-old self to approach my mom to ask her what happened.

I entered my parents' room one morning, where my

mom was lying on the foot of her bed watching television. "Mommy, what happened to Daddy?"

"What do you mean, honey?"

"Well, he's different," I remarked.

"What do you mean different? Good different or bad different?" she questioned.

"Good different!" I exclaimed. "What happened?"

What happened next was a whirlwind of amazing goodness. My mother took the time to patiently explain to me that they, my mom and dad, had found Jesus and that Daddy had asked Jesus to be his Lord and Savior. With peace like a river pressing in around me, I knew immediately that I wanted Jesus too! So that day, at age six, I prayed with my mom and asked Jesus to come and take over my life too. He did just that, and I have never looked back. It was the best decision of my life. It always will be the very best and most important decision I have ever made, no matter what else may come along.

After that morning in my parents' room, the real "eating" and "growing" transformation began. I wanted to be baptized immediately (once I was told what that meant). So, a family friend that became very influential in my faith walk baptized me, my cousins, my uncle, and my daddy, and I began to learn about the thrilling awesomeness of God. I began "heavy lifting" in the faith arena, as it were.

Now, at age seven, I had an insatiable appetite for God and His word, so I read the Bible and pondered it, devouring the words by reading as much of it as I could each night, after crawling into bed all snuggled down under my warm blankets. I listened as my family and church leaders talked, lived, and taught its truths in front of me. The simplest and most difficult of tasks could not be too hard for the God of the Bible that I was learning about and personally getting to know. Personally! Yes! This is not an expression or phrase, this is literal. So many people think that God is far away, or is too busy doing other big things to listen to us and build a personal relationship. This is simply not so. God is God. He can do anything and everything all at once while still having a relationship with you. Actually, if we let Him, God is fun, intimate, detailed, big, and loving all at the same time.

My next skin-shedding event was actually a series of many spectacular events all piled into my life, one after another. Kind of like a snowball effect, growing larger with each passing moment as gravitational momentum pulls it along. But this next specific event that took place in my life shows God's intimate and meticulously loving character, even toward a little girl.

After being "saved," I was still a child, so I naturally thought like a child. Young, innocent, and often a bit ridiculous and silly. One day I got the bright idea that I wanted bluebonnets. Okay, y'all, I'm from Texas. Bluebonnets are our state flower, and in my opinion are beautiful with their tiny blue petals and pristine white "bonnets" that sit on top. Nothing says spring like sitting in a large field of bluebonnets and having your picture taken over and over again. I wanted bluebonnets and was telling my mom all about my desire before school one morning. We lived in a two-story brick house in the Chesterfield subdivision of Katy, Texas, where the corner lot next to us sat empty and full of weeds. I called that lot next to our driveway "the field."

"Mommy, I want bluebonnets. Wouldn't it be great if our whole field were filled with them? Then we could go run and play in a big field of bluebonnets. Doesn't that sound like fun?" I chattered as we walked toward our car parked under the porte cochere.

My mom, Marti, patiently listened to me talking about these bluebonnets when I suddenly decided something. "I know, I'll ask God for some bluebonnets! He makes the flowers, so He can make some for me."

My mom looked at me with those loving mommy eyes that said, "Don't be too disappointed when your prayer doesn't come true."

We were all new to walking with God, and He was busy building all of our faith, not just mine. Even with that "hope you don't get too sad" look from my mom, I decided to exercise my childish faith in my creator for whom I had been learning nothing was too big or too small. I just KNEW that He would answer my prayer. So, what did I do? I ran down our driveway to our mailbox and told God that I wanted bluebonnets. Standing next to our mailbox, I prayed, "Dear God, could I please have three bluebonnets next to our mailbox so I will know they are from you?" Then I pointed to the ground and said, "Right here. Thank you." I smiled up at the expansive blue sky above and ran back to my mom, my sneakers slapping on the pavement, so she could drive me to school.

The day continued on in typical manner. I went to school. I learned something, or maybe just daydreamed through my classes, as I was so prone to doing. I had a bad habit of going to school and zoning out during class while my teachers droned on about whatever subject I was supposed to be listening to. Quite often, I would be asked a question multiple times and end up just staring at the teacher in blank confusion. The world going on in my imagination was much more interesting than the math or history lesson in my textbook. Every time the bell rang, signaling us to switch classes, I had to climb out of a haze of thoughts in order to gather my supplies into my backpack and not be late to my next class.

My mom most likely ran around town, trying to complete her typical errands of grocery shopping and other necessary ventures, before heading back to the school to pick me up. Just another typical day. That is until God showed up.

As we drove home, I listened to the tires humming on the pavement and nearly nodded off to sleep, but as soon as I felt the car bump over the end of the driveway, I remembered my prayer to God that morning. Once the car was safely parked, I ran down to my mailbox, my hair blowing in front of my face. I nearly tripped over my own feet because I simply could not get there fast enough. I leaned over panting, prepared to take a good long look at my three bluebonnets that I just KNEW God had given to me. And, there they were! Three perfectly beautiful blue flowers bejeweled in their white caps and bright green leaves.

Now, I know what you are thinking: my mom didn't want my heart to be broken, so she went out and bought those bluebonnets and planted them there for me. Guess what? God knew I would be writing this book, and that you would think that, so He took care of that little detail for us too.

"Mommy! Mommy! Guess what?" I was giggling and screaming for my mom, running halfway up the driveway toward her and back down to the fresh flowers by the mailbox again, unsure of where exactly I should go. I was so excited about these three pretty, full-grown flowers by my mailbox that I simply didn't know how to react.

My mom jumped outside the car, no doubt thinking that something must be wrong from all of my running back and forth coupled with the squeals and screaming coming from my mouth, but then she stopped frozen, struck with awe, shock, and who knows what other emotions. She was stuck in her tracks, seemingly unable to move or speak for a moment.

Once she regained her senses, she said, "Yes. Yes, Natalie. I see your three bluebonnets, but look! God didn't stop there. Look! Look at our field!" She stretched her hand out before her, pointing to the miracle that sat waiting to be enjoyed.

The field, the empty corner lot next to our house was full of full-grown bluebonnets. Hundreds of flowers that had not been there earlier that day. The field that had been nothing but prairie grass and weeds before school that morning was now filled with perfectly beautiful bluebonnets, whose white-bonneted heads were nodding and winking in the wind as if to say, "Yes, He put us here for you."

No dug-up dirt, no tricks, no man-made design from the garden store...just a glorious, faith-building gift from God.

If that doesn't show how God is into details, doesn't show His extravagance, all for a child to build her faith in Him, being able to do the big and small things, then I don't know what does. He built my faith that day. He built my parents' faith that day too.

I wasn't just a young eating caterpillar anymore; I was starting to gain some spiritual fat, the laying of a foundation in Him.

THREE

A NEW SCHOOL

And my God will meet all your needs according to the riches of His glory in Christ Jesus.

PHILIPPIANS 4:19
(NIV)

Earlier I mentioned that this time in my life was full of a series of many spectacular events all heaped together. And it was. The bluebonnet story is just one small story of the many times God was showing up in my family's life during this newness of a relationship with Him. The stories of Him working and showing up in my life would fill a book of its own, and maybe I will write that one day, but for this book, I will share just a few more of those stories to help give you an idea of my caterpillar years of "eating" and "shedding" and "growing" that took place in the "pre-cocoon" years of my life.

Because of these many faith-filled life instances, I walked with a simple faith. I simply believed. This next story of faith was a leap for my parents, and it is how I ended up in a private Christian school.

I was in 5th grade when my family went through a move. We were struggling financially and needed to make a big change to help pay the bills. God provided in an immense way for that change to take place but, still, the change was hard. We had to sell many of our belongings, box up what remained and move into a much smaller house than we were used to. We moved to a different area of town, and I had to change schools in the middle of my 5th-grade year. It was horrendous! Not the "switching schools" part, but the new school I ended up going to.

I had moved fairly often as a child of parents that built houses in the Houston, Texas, area for a living. Construction was so fun and interesting to me. Moving was just part of the territory. As a homebuilder, my dad often built a few spec homes that would sit on the market for sale. My family would live in one of the homes, and it was always the house we lived in that sold. My mom was an expert at keeping our house looking like a model home, even with us living in it. So, naturally, it was easier for the buyer to "imagine" their belongings there instead of in one of the empty spec homes. We would sell that house, box up, and move to one of the other houses we had in inventory, and repeat until we stayed in one for a while.

Even though we would often move houses, we always stayed in the same town and close to family. Often times a move meant I had to change schools, but we usually moved in the summer, so I don't ever remember changing locations in the middle of a school year before. I liked change, so it didn't bother me. New schools, teachers, and friends were an exciting adventure.

This move was different. There was a financial crash

going on and my dad had sold all of his houses. We were in desperate need of a home to live in, and God provided a place for us at the very last moment. This time I was ten years old, in the 5th grade, and we moved in the middle of the school year. Naturally, I had to go to a new school. No big deal, right? Wrong!

This new school was not like anything I had been to before. Many of the kids were gang members, and all kinds of things that a ten-year-old should not know about were going on in the bathrooms between classes. The atmosphere of the school was filled with entitlement, heaviness, and fear. Many students and teachers looked the other way when bad things were happening, so as not to end up on the radar of a local gang. It was all immorality and Godlessness. Shadows lurked in the halls searching for their next prey as dim lights flickered instead of staying brightly lit for students to find their way.

I remember having to stand up for a very pretty, petite girl who caught the eye of a local gang leader. I stuck to her like glue so she didn't have to "visit the bathroom" with one of the boys. After that day paired up with her, I became ill. Very physically sick. I couldn't tell you exactly what was wrong with me, but the symptoms included me not being able to get out of bed. My parents could not get me back to school. I was weak and depressed. My stomach was upset, and I couldn't eat. I just wanted to sleep all the time.

After about two weeks of illness, with no end in sight, and no true diagnosis as to what was ailing me, my doctor suggested writing a prescription to send me back to my old school to finish out the year. I was instantly better and back to my old self. The oppression had been too heavy where I was but lifted the moment I was able to leave that dark and demonic atmosphere. Yes, we are supposed to be a light in a dark world, but that particular location had no desire to look into the light of Jesus I carried around with me.

Logically, the next year I would have had to go to the junior high that the offending elementary school fed into, but the rumors of the local junior high school were even worse than what I had experienced at the elementary school. No way was I going to go there after the experience I had in 5th grade.

One day, during the summer and after graduating elementary school, I informed my parents of my new plan. "Daddy, Mommy, I'm going to go to the private school at our church next year." I made this announcement and walked away like it was a done deal. Oops! Wait a minute. My parents were in a financially difficult time and private schools were expensive.

"Natalie," my dad responded while following me out of the room, "you do realize that there is a monthly tuition, right? And we would also have to buy uniforms and books and pay for any extra sports, right? That all costs money...money we don't have."

"If God wants me to go there, He will provide the money," I stated matter-of-factly, and I walked away a second time.

That was it. As far as I was concerned, God wanted me to go to Faith West Academy in Katy, Texas, so He would quite easily provide the money. No stress, no worry, no concern at all. Well, I was only ten, so of course there was no stress for me. For my parents...well, you would have to ask them, but now that I am a parent myself, I am sure they felt the full stress of the situation.

They faced the stress head-on and did what they have always done: they prayed. We moved forward with the enrollment forms, student interviews, and entrance testing for Faith West, standing on faith and a little bit of trepidation.

I remember my interview with the principal. I was so nervous. Looking back, I'm not really sure why I was so nervous since I wasn't an unruly child, but the idea of sitting in front of a man—a principal—and answering questions made my stomach quiver and my palms sweaty. Even though my parents were in the room with me, and even though I went to church with this principal and spoke with him regularly in "normal life," I felt a little lightheaded as he spoke with me in this particular school entrance interview.

"Will you be obedient when the teachers ask you to do something?" Mr. Tankersley queried.

"Yes," I whispered while looking down at the floor.

"Will you do your work to the best of your ability?"

"Uh-hum, yes." I nodded without making eye contact.

"You do know that your response should be 'yes, sir' or 'yes, ma'am,' don't you?" Mr. Tankersley chuckled.

"Yes." My voice cracked.

"Yes what?" He laughed with a twinkle in his eye.

I blinked and looked at him. He laughed again while staring at me. I must have been turning pale or green as I began tilting to the side and sliding out of my chair.

"Yes what?" Mr. Tankersley asked again.

Pause.

"Um. Yes, sir?" I questioned.

"Exactly!" he exclaimed. "You passed your interview, welcome to our school!"

And wouldn't you know that when the first tuition check was due, my dad got an extra job contract, not through his home-building efforts, for those had ceased for the time being, but rather through his small roofing company. And those extra contracts continued to roll in each month for the next six years (I graduated a year early). Whenever we needed to buy uniforms, pay for books or sports, or even pay the standard tuition, the money was always there, and we still never missed a meal. God provided, and not just once, but month after month after month. Thank you, God, you met our needs.

FOUR

BUG COLLECTION

*Every good and perfect gift is from above, coming
down from the Father of the heavenly lights, who
does not change like shifting shadows.*

JAMES 1:17
(NIV)

Junior High Science Class. Objective: Bug
Collection.

I apologize up front to all the bug lovers out there,
but in junior high we had to assemble a bug collection. And
I (*gasp!*) killed bugs! Hey, I was a kid, so I actually thought it
was a really cool project. Although I was full of fascination
over these creepy-crawlies, I did cry several times during the
process of actually tacking a particularly large insect onto
my science board, so I'm not completely heartless.

Our assignment was to collect a specific number of
insects, pin them to a board, appropriately labeled, and give

an oral dissertation on the collection by a specific date. I was eleven or twelve years old at the time.

Finding bugs here in Texas is not very difficult. With the high humidity and hot weather, they seem to be everywhere. Usually where a person didn't want them to be. Just look in the corner of the garage for dead cockroaches (*yuck!*), or pick mushrooms and store them in a plastic bag until the domed insect home is vacated and the occupants are fully departed. Simply going for a walk in the evening ensures you become a mosquito meal. Mosquitoes here in Texas are the size of small birds, so this is another great way to catch said project requirements.

I had my project assembled fairly quickly due to the over-abundance of multilegged creatures in my locality, but there was one bug I still wanted and simply could not figure out how to acquire him. The elusive green darner is a particularly stunning dragonfly, and I wanted it for the center of my board. It can grow up to three inches in length and is a brilliant bright green. Its eyes are huge and simply mesmerizing. I really didn't want to kill one of these creatures, but I did want to stare at it and have it as a trophy of God's beautiful creation on my bug board. Que sera, sera! After trying to catch a few with no success, my parents got involved and the catching of the green darner became a family affair.

In this new family effort to complete "The Bug Board," my dad bought a bug net and we kept a lookout everywhere we went. We even pulled over to the side of the road a few times to chase a swarm of the mysterious iridescent dragonflies. They always flew away. Then, one weekend, my dad had the great idea of going to a cemetery. You know—trees, nature, and bugs.

Jackpot! They were everywhere. Swarms and swarms of

them flying high up in the air, then suddenly swooping down to dive-bomb mosquitoes as a favorite meal. The chase was on. Okay, stop! Before you get the crazy image in your mind of us running around all over gravesites, we did NOT run (or walk) on the graves. There were large, unused fields at the cemetery too and that is where we ran around, completely undignified, trying to catch dragonflies. We left the tombs alone.

Imagine this: we would run with the net raised in the air above our heads and yell "Jesus" like He would put one in our net for us. It was so fun! And I'm sure it was a hilarious sight to behold. Alas, even with all of the running, yelling, and chasing, we came home empty-handed. No green darner fainted in mid-flight only to fall into our bug net.

On another day, my mom decided to go to a truck stop nearby and scour the semitrucks' front grilles in the hope of finding a dead darner trapped in the muck. Genius. And yes, as gross as this sounds, it really did happen. Picture a lovely mom, all dolled up in her cute hairstyle and makeup, leaning over to inspect truck grille after truck grille. Although I have no idea what manner of squished and oozing insects she may have encountered that day, none of them was a green darner. At least none of them were recognizable as one.

With the bug project almost due, I was one insect short of a full science board. With only a few days left and little to show for all our roadside, graveyard, and truck stop traipsing, I began to feel discouraged and wondered if I might fail the project altogether. So, now what? Oh wait, haven't I been building faith these past four to five years? Maybe I should pray? Can I even pray for a bug to come be killed for my science project? I was, after all, more mature, not a seven-year-old asking for bluebonnets. Hmm...well, God says to pray and ask Him, so that is what I did. I prayed, but this time it was my mom that God wanted to surprise. After all, she had been searching and praying for this bug too.

What happened? Another day at school is what happened. Yup. My mom dropped me off at school, just like always. Only now that I was at the private school, I no longer daydreamed through my classes. I actually listened, learned, and tried. I discovered that school was actually hard, challenging, and good mental exercise. I now took pleasure in learning.

Meanwhile, my mom prayed, just like always. She lives a life of prayer and prays about everything...including bug projects. And you know what happened? God listened!

On her way home from dropping me off at school that warm and sunny morning, the biggest most spectacular green darner got its wing caught in the crack between the hood and the body of her car. It was stuck there and simply rode home with her. No bug net needed. No jumping or yelling, no graveyard (although I must admit that was riotously fun) and no plans or schemes either. God simply caught this dragonfly and hand delivered him to my mom's car. I'm guessing it was an old bug simply by the sheer size of it. I believe that it had lived a long and satisfying life and was now on its way out, so God escorted it to us. When my mom arrived home, she got out of the car, scooped up the perfectly intact dragonfly, and set it aside for me.

The school day came to an end, and when my mom brought me home that afternoon, she had the funniest grin on her face.

"Natalie, guess what God did today?" She was nearly bursting with anticipation, wanting to blurt out all the details.

"I don't know, what?" I replied.

"Oh come on, can't you guess? I know, let's play Twenty Questions," my mom teased. Twenty Questions was my mom's favorite game to play when she wanted to reveal something but still make it fun.

"Okay, is it bigger than a bread box?" I quizzed.

"No." She smirked.

"Can it fly?" I queried.

"Yes and no," she replied.

"Is it alive?" I wondered aloud.

"Yes and no." She giggled.

"Okay, I give up. What is it?"

"Look!" She pulled a jar out from behind her back. And there it was—that wondrous green darner as the trophy bug for the middle of my science board.

That's how God works. He is fun and spontaneous. He is a good gift giver. And He bolstered our faith and added another layer of fat and foundation to our lives. All because He can, and He loves us. And you know what? None of us have ever had a fully intact dragonfly ride home with us on our car since. Only God.

FIVE

RUNNING

Therefore, since we are surrounded by such a great cloud of witnesses, let us throw off everything that hinders and the sin that so easily entangles. And let us run with perseverance the race marked out for us, fixing our eyes on Jesus, the pioneer and perfecter of faith. For the joy set before Him He endured the cross, scorning its shame, and sat down at the right hand of the throne of God.

HEBREWS 12:1-2
(NIV)

These fun, cool, and childish interactions with the Lord was His kind way to meet me, a child, where I was. He was growing me into who I would become. He was whispering in my ear that He cares, He is listening, He is always there. He was walking with me and nothing was too small or silly for Him.

This relationship allowed me to be open and transparent with my savior. Training me to lean on Him, so that when I would inevitably really need Him, I would not waver, collapse, or second-guess His goodness. Teaching me to follow Him so I would move ahead with bold purpose even in the trial ahead. My childish faith and relationship with God deepened over the years into a mature and intimate faith full of longing and trust.

Before I dive into the next story of faith, I want to take an interlude and tell you about how I became a runner. Running was a love for me that I eventually mourned the loss of. Many of you reading this may have lost something near to your heart too but know that it can be restored.

Prior to the age of fifteen, I hated running. I repeat: I hated, loathed, despised (and all other negative adjectives you can think of) running. I had struggled with asthma as a youngster but seemed to slowly outgrow that breathing issue. In elementary school, my one-mile-run time was always one of the slowest, clocking in between thirteen and fifteen minutes per mile. If I hadn't been dragged along by one of my friends, I'm sure my mile time would have been near the twenty-minute mark; more of a leisurely walk time. I would walk/run—walk a little, then run a little. I hated the pounding of my feet on the ground and the ache of my knees as I propelled myself forward. I never knew what to do with my hands, and my hair would whip around in my ponytail and slap me in the face with every bounce of my step.

You know those people that look pretty when they run? I was not one of them. My face would turn bright red with dull green blotches, like a badly decorated Christmas wreath. My hair would fall out of its ponytail and try to wrap its sticky tendrils around my neck to strangle me. I didn't sweat, per se, but I would glisten just enough to feel clammy and uncomfortable. Good thing I wasn't too concerned about my running time because I had no plans on ever becoming a professional runner.

I could, however, jump. I could jump high and I could jump far. In the standing broad jump, I always jumped about six inches longer than my height, and that was without practice or training. That was just showing up on the day of the test and taking a big standing jump. This ability to jump when I was only 5' 3" tall helped me to do well when playing volleyball with my friends in junior high. Of course, part of volleyball training was running laps around the hot, humid gym. Grueling! I persevered, but that was my least favorite part. What I didn't realize was that I was building up stamina after running volleyball laps over and over again. Not speed, because I never pushed myself to go faster than a thirteen-minute mile, but stamina and I were becoming friends.

During my sophomore year of high school, I decided I would try out for cheerleading. I still went to a private Christian school, so even as cheerleaders we dressed more conservatively for a squad, and our dance moves were "mom approved." Plus, I knew I could jump, so why not try out? The worst that could happen was I wouldn't make the squad.

I remember everyone was shocked that I even wanted to go out for the squad. I was the quiet girl that almost never spoke and had only played a little volleyball. I was also the "Goody Two-shoes," so to speak, never getting into trouble or attracting attention to myself. For the life of me, I still don't know why I was so determined to try out, but it just seemed fun to me. Cheerleading was something to do to make more friends and be part of a team. And I could jump.

As part of making the team, I was told I had to run an

eight-and-a-half-minute mile. In the words of Scooby-Doo: "Ruh-roh!" This was a little startling. I had never run faster than a thirteen-minute mile. Ever! But then again, I had never tried to run a fast mile, so who knew? I decided to team up with a girl who I knew could run the mile in eight minutes flat, and simply kept my stride right behind her. I felt fine running and didn't push myself. I listened to the rhythm of my shoes slapping the floor. I mimicked the way she held her hands and swung her arms. I giggled, laughed, and encouraged the other girls running around me. I finished my first mile in seven minutes and forty-eight seconds, and I wasn't even winded or tired. Actually, I felt great. I had some serious happy endorphins flooding my bloodstream and wanted to keep going. Maybe this running thing wasn't so bad after all. But even with that great mile time, I still didn't know I could run.

After tryouts I found that I made the cheer squad. I also got my first boyfriend (which was not the goal of being a cheerleader) and enjoyed my sophomore year.

One Wednesday, my new boyfriend, Jay, my parents, and I went out to eat together after school. After our early dinner, my parents drove us "kids" back to Faith West so we would be there for youth group that night. Being both a church and a private school, Faith West was always busy and full of friends. When we hopped out of my dad's truck, we could see Jay's car from across the parking lot, and it looked strange. We couldn't really see what was wrong with it, but gazing at it from across the lot we could tell there was definitely something different.

"Something is wrong with my car!" Jay yelled.

"I'll go check it out," I affirmed as I turned and began running across the lot. Jay and some of the other guys hanging around the area took off, sprinting toward the car at the same time I did.

When I reached the car ahead of them, I turned around and yelled back, "It's fine, nothing to worry about, just a silly prank with window chalk. It'll wash off."

A moment later, the guys came wheezing and panting up to me and declared the situation safe. I hadn't even realized that I had outrun the guys until my dad and our track coach came meandering over talking to each other. Apparently, they both saw me sprint whatever distance it was.

Coach always had his whistle around his neck and his stopwatch on his wrist. "You made great time there, Natalie," he proclaimed.

"Well...okay...yes, sir. Coach. I just ran to a car," I said.

"I think you should come try out for the track team," Coach stated, and my dad nodded.

"Um. Sure, whatever." I shrugged.

No, not whatever. The next week I found myself on the track team, being placed into the preseason cross-country team. We didn't have any meets at this time, just a lot of training. I never did get to run in a meet because several months later, just before the training period slowed down and the actual meets began, I tore the tendons and ligaments in my ankle. I will never forget that day in the gym.

Being a small school, the guys and girls both shared the workout room. We had a weight and workout routine that we stuck to in order to stay fit and ready for whatever sports we happened to be in, so all the different athletes used the room together. That particular day, I had done my arm routine and was moving on to the core workout. I climbed up onto the power tower to complete my hanging leg-ups and ab workouts. Christian music was blaring. Teenagers were talking and metal was clanging as weights were being removed and replaced from the racks and machines around the room. When I was done with my ab routine, I stepped down off the high machine and heard pop, pop, pop, pop. The sound was so loud and unnatural that everyone working out in the gym stopped what they were doing, and all eyes turned toward me.

I looked at their faces and just stood there on one foot, unsure of what to do. I knew my ankle had made those noises. I had felt the searing, cutting pain rip through my foot. My relationship with Jay had already fizzled out, and I had actually begun dating one of my best friends for the past five years, Shane. My wide eyes found Shane's face and pleaded for help. Then I took a tentative step toward the door and collapsed into his arms. That was the end of my track career; over before it had even begun.

Before that missed first track meet and destroying almost all of the tendons and ligaments in my ankle, I had lots of practice with the team. I sat the bench that season and cheered from the sidelines but I chose not to try out again the next year.

What I did learn before I tore up my ankle, and after I recovered, was that I loved running long distances. I was too fast to run with the girls, so a few of the guys slowed down a bit for me and we would go on long runs together each day. We would run anywhere from five to ten miles for fun and just joke around, then during the last mile the guys would pick up their speed and leave me in the dust.

I averaged a 6:19 mile in those days and always felt peaceful, like I was flying. I also used my solo runs to worship the Lord and commune with Him. I've always felt closest to my God when I'm in His nature, and running long distances gave me that precious nature time alone with Him.

SIX

ANGELS

For He shall give His angels charge over you, to keep you in all your ways. In their hands they shall bear you up, lest you dash your foot against a stone.

PSALM 91:11-12

(NKJV)

A year later I was sixteen years old and still going to Faith West. Faith West was a wonderful church and private school community. I had very strong friendships, many of which are still intact today. We went to church together, played sports together, ate, hung out, worked, and even studied together. The whole group of us. We were rarely alone, and we functioned more like a family than classmates or church friends. I was still very much the quiet observer type of a person but had become more outgoing as a cheerleader. My relationship with the Lord had also deepened. I recognized His voice. My spirit had become very sensitive and in tune with my God.

Not only did I speak to Him and pray often, but He communicated with me. I had spiritual dreams and visions, I heard His voice and I often just had a knowing when He would speak to me. This was normal for me, not some rare weekend thing that happened only on Sundays, but a nearly constant line of communication between my Lord and myself. Yes, I was still an imperfect teenager, but I also tried to be quick to repent or ask forgiveness when I did something that I recognized as wrong. I was growing, but not grown. I still needed to shed my caterpillar skin before I would be ready for what lay ahead.

Every Wednesday night we had youth group. This was a time in the evening when us teenagers would get together with our youth leader and play, worship, and learn about God. It was a safe place for us to be us. An environment where we were nurtured in the Lord and trained how to grow in life, all while the rigid boundaries of school and normal everyday existence was loosened. We would hang out some more after our Bible study time and play music, pool, cards, basketball or whatever was good clean fun at the time, and then we would part ways for the evening, just to do it all over again the next week.

Our youth group had a special place that we built just for us "youths." We had loud music, colored lights, a fish tank inside an old television set, crazy knickknacks hanging from the ceiling and stuck in the walls, and a coffee/smoothie bar. We also had a pool table, card games, and lounging furniture. The walls were decorated with funky putty and colored glass rocks. Everything teenagers needed to be relaxed and goofy, more mature yet still young and silly. It was our safe haven to ask the difficult questions and not be judged harshly by those that could hurt us.

One particular Wednesday, we had our typical youth

group meeting. After hanging out for a while, I said bye to my friends and Shane. After our goodbyes, I headed outside to my car while the others stayed in to hang out longer. It was dark outside as the sun set earlier in the fall than in the summer months. I got all the way into my car—a small bright blue Ford Escort ZX2 coupe—and started the engine, when I suddenly heard God tell me to go back inside and tell my boyfriend to pray for my safety on the way home.

It would have been really easy to ignore that internal voice and just drive home. The engine was already running, and I could feel the vibrations of the car waiting for me to put it into drive. But I knew God. I knew His promptings and I listened. I also had a very understanding boyfriend that took seriously the promptings the Holy Spirit often gave me. Shane never sloughed those prompt-ings off, never teased me or called me ridiculous. Rather, he honored God himself by listening. So, I took the one or two minutes of hassle it took to run in and ask him to pray while I would be driving home. He prayed and I drove away. Of course, I was also praying. Nothing particular, but mostly that God would keep me safe on the way home and post His angels on the hood and trunk of my car.

The path from the church to my home had one particu-larly dangerous stretch of road, but at night it was usually empty of any other vehicles. This road was fairly new construction and very dark at night, with a fifty-miles-per-hour speed limit. Smaller roads turned on to this main thor-oughfare from stop signs. There were no stoplights or street-lights yet, only a vehicle's headlights to brighten the path ahead. This path would become inky black, and this night was no exception. Even though it was so dark, I didn't give this road much thought because I was so used to driving it every day—to and from school during the week, and to church on Sundays.

I was flying down the unlit roadway at fifty miles per hour when suddenly a huge dually truck turned from one of those shadowy stop signs and took the very spot my car was in, or had been in. I did not have time to hit the brakes. I didn't swerve or slow down. I didn't even have the chance to scream. I simply felt the sudden sensation of my car being lifted into the air and gently set down about fifteen feet to the right, onto the grassy shoulder beside the road. I saw the dually truck now speeding where my car once was. I sat stunned and a bit bewildered in my driver's seat, being physically jostled back and forth as the body of my car rocked on its tires. The crunch of gravel ground in my ears as the truck that had taken my vehicle's former spot on the road proceeded to spin its wheels, spit rocks, and speed down the dark roadway, swerving and being driven reck-lessly. I am pretty sure the driver was either drunk or high, and I was a rescued casualty.

I sat there in the dark for several minutes, breathing hard and thanking God, before being able to meander back on to the roadway and travel the rest of the way home. What just happened? God happened. Angels lifted my car, moved it to the side, and saved my life.

Apparently, I had more life to live. Obviously, we were supposed to pray for a reason. Had I left initially, instead of going back inside to ask for prayer, I would have been a mere few minutes in front of a reckless driver that was swerving through dark roadways at speeds much higher than the traffic laws permitted. Had I not asked for prayer and prayed myself, the angels may not have moved me out of the way. I may have been rear-ended or sideswiped and lying crumpled dead in a mangled mass of metal. Yes, God can do anything, but He uses our participation and obedience. Prayer is part of that. God was showing Himself to me again. He is real, alive, and in communication with me.

I had now shed my caterpillar skin again and was getting quite large and fat.

SEVEN

LEAVE NOW

For no prophecy was ever produced by the will of man, but men spoke from God as they were carried along by the Holy Spirit.

2 PETER 1:21
(ESV)

My sheep hear My voice, and I know them, and they follow Me. And I give them eternal life, and they shall never perish; neither shall anyone snatch them out of My hand.

JOHN 10:27-28
(NKJV)

G od talks. Daily if we will listen. At first His speaking may seem distant or quiet; some people call it a sixth sense or a knowing. As in, I sensed something was going to happen before it did, or I knew something was wrong with *xyz*. People tend to go through life "following their gut." Yes, I do believe we should pay attention to that whisper of caution that sometimes comes, but I also consider that we must realize that many times the small quiet voice or knowing that we experience, that sixth sense or gut feeling, is actually God speaking to us. Not always, but often.

Don't get all "knowings" or "voices" confused. There are two sides to the spiritual coin. There is God, but there is also an enemy. The enemy speaks too. Remember, God will never ask us to do something that contradicts His Word, the Bible. God is love, so if you think you are hearing God tell you to do something that opposes love, then it is not God. The more you build your relationship with the One True God, the easier it is to recognize His voice and discern it from your own thoughts, or something else.

I was seventeen years old, and when I wasn't with one of my best friends Kelly or Beth, I was glued at the hip to Shane. We did almost everything together, probably to the chagrin of both our friends and parents, but hey...teenagers in love. Those were the best years of my youthful life. Sure, there were a roller coaster of emotions involved, as with any young relationship, but we had so much fun with each other and the group of friends we were growing up with. I was so carefree and enjoyed life to the fullest. Or at least I tired.

Through one of our friend's connections, we began working as volunteers for Christian concerts, alongside our local Christian radio station KSBJ. We did this for several years and worked countless concerts all around town. Some were in small churches and others were in large sports arenas, including the Astrodome, but most were in a location built specifically for outdoor concerts, the Cynthia Woods Mitchell Pavilion.

We did everything from picking up band members at their hotels, setting up equipment, helping the side shows prepare, selling memorabilia, praying for concertgoers and more. We were on stage, off stage, behind stage, in the crowd and anywhere else we were needed at any given moment. We arrived extra early to help set up before the concerts started and left extra late, usually after teardown was complete. It was fast, loud, bright, crowded, exhausting...an overwhelming buffet for the senses, and I wouldn't have changed a single moment. Not only was it exciting, but it also filled my spirit to overflowing. I treasured being surrounded by worship music, Christian rock/pop and other genres that lifted up the name of Jesus. I cherished meeting so many spirit-filled believers, band members, pastors, and like-minded teenagers. I felt free, vibrant, and alive. The work was long and hard, but the reward was great.

We would typically finish helping with the teardown and either go eat at a late-night breakfast restaurant like I-HOP (it could easily be 1 or 2 a.m.), or just head home if we were completely smashed. This night was the latter. We were smashed. We had been working a concert at the Cynthia Woods Mitchell Pavilion in the Woodlands, and it was so late that Shane and I decided we needed to head back across town toward home in Katy. This was before the Grand Parkway connected everything, so the drive was lengthy. Shane always drove us wherever we needed to go; he had picked me up at my house earlier in the day and was my ride home when the event ended. The drive usually took a bit longer than an hour, and it was already around 1 a.m. While we were on the road, he realized we were running dangerously low on gasoline. We needed to stop at the next station to fill up.

"There's a station up ahead. Let's just pull in there, fill up, and get home," Shane said.

"Yeah, sounds good. I'm tired," I replied.

So, he pulled up to the pump, rolled down our windows, opened the door to the gas tank, and pulled out the nozzle when suddenly I heard a voice YELL in my heart.

"Leave now. You are in danger. Leave!"

This voice was so loud I jumped in my seat. My heart rate sped up and my hands began to tremble. Shane had yet to put a single drop of gasoline into the car, but I leaned toward his window anyway. "We have to leave. Now." My voice was calm, but he immediately sensed the urgency in my eyes.

"Now?" he questioned with that probing look he would get like he was searching my soul to read what was going on inside my head. I gave one firm nod and watched as he replaced the gas pump nozzle, hearing it scrape as the metal connected back into its cradle. He climbed into the car and we left.

Once we were safe on the road, he glanced at me from the corner of his eyes. "Why did we have to leave?"

"God was yelling inside my head. He said we had to leave now, that we were in danger. I didn't want to take any chances, and with the sudden chills that took over my body, I knew we should listen."

At first I thought Shane might think I was crazy and let me know it, but he had been so faithful to listen in the past that I wasn't surprised when he just gave me a look of belief and kept his eyes open for the next gas station. We found one, filled up, and finally made the rest of our weary trek home.

Once home, Shane escorted me inside. My dad was still awake, lounging in his recliner listening to the news. He was always up late, so this was typical, but this time the news caught my attention. It was breaking news. The first gas station Shane and I had so abruptly fled had a fatal shooting take place just minutes after we had left.

I started trembling with adrenaline and thoughts of "that could have been us." We both started stumbling all over our words, trying to tell my dad what had happened.

In typical dad fashion, he said, "Well, I'm glad you're safe. I'm going to bed. Good night."

"He took that in stride, don't you think?" I mumbled. My boyfriend and I took a moment to thank God for His prompting and our safety. Then I made Shane promise to call me as soon as he arrived safely home.

This was a faith-building moment. I was not just an "eating" and "skin-shedding" caterpillar anymore. I was a fat caterpillar about ready for the cocoon.

EIGHT

COLLEGE

*You can make many plans, but the Lord's purpose
will prevail.*

PROVERBS 19:21
(NLT)

L ife took the natural course of events, with high school
coming to an end and the college years beginning. I
was so ready for college that I decided to finish senior year
of high school at a "go at your own pace" private school so I
could graduate in December 1997 instead of May 1998.

I had cherished school, but over time I became tired of
high school and a bit jaded of its clique-ish drama. At the
age of seventeen, I moved on to college. Honestly, college
was difficult for me. I enjoyed the social aspect and living
semi-independently, but I struggled relentlessly in all of my
non-science or non-math classes that had no pertinence
toward my microbiology major. Making the grade was
tremendously difficult for me in the boring and mundane

classes that were completely unrelated to the sciences. Classes like English and economics ate my lunch. I spent many nights shedding tears over my textbooks as I attempted to absorb and make sense of what on earth these nonsensical classes were trying to advise me.

My original plan was to go to Houston Baptist University to major in microbiology and minor in nursing, but through a strange series of events, I changed plans. I started off at Houston Community College the January after graduation, for my first semester of classes and a summer session, before transferring over to Texas A&M University. My experience at Texas A&M was not my favorite; I should have stuck with Houston Baptist for the long haul. I struggled to find like-minded friends and the professors seemed to not really care or lecture well (at least in my freshman, non-science classes). My roommate brought her boyfriend over for "sleepovers" in our tiny, one-room shared living space, even though she knew I didn't approve, and I had a stalker that tried to terrify me on more than one occasion.

Many times, I would come back to my apartment from an evening church service to receive a phone call from an unknown male voice asking me where I had been. Or I would leave my classes during the day to find a note on my car letting me know "he" was watching me. This stalking went on for quite some time, and the response was always "no" whenever I asked others if they had seen who had tampered with my vehicle.

One night I had been to a church service, and as soon as I entered my apartment, my phone rang.

"Hello," I answered.

"Where have you been?" a deep hostile voice questioned.

"Who is this?" I demanded, with a useless stomp of my foot.

"That is none of your business. What I will tell you is that you are getting home too late. Where have you been? Who were you with?" the voice slowly enunciated.

"I was at church!" I loudly declared, and promptly hung up on this unwelcome intruder.

I threw open my door and gazed around the night-darkened courtyard to see if I could spy anyone from a nearby apartment looking through his window at me. Nothing. There weren't even any lights on in other windows. I began to pray and prepare; I felt something more was coming.

R-I-N-G.

My phone began to scream again.

"What do you want?" I answered.

"I want you!" the young man's voice seethed through the airwaves. "You hung up on me. I've been keeping my eye on you. Keeping you safe, and this is how you repay me?"

My skin began to crawl, and my body shivered, as fear and uncertainty crept into my mind.

"You won't even tell me who you are. That is not a relationship!" I stated, with bravado I currently did not feel, before slamming the phone down on him again.

After that show of bravado, I marched over to my neighbors' door and pounded on it thinking that the two guys who lived there may have been playing a prank on me. They were super confused when they answered my hammering and swore that they had not been calling or following me. With that unsatisfactory response, I marched down the long dark outdoor corridor to the apartment's main office and requested to see my incoming phone records.

"Excuse me, can I get a list of calls coming to my room?" I questioned as politely as I could.

"Sorry, but we don't have that type of information," the sonorous male receptionist behind the desk advised me.

"You don't understand! Someone is stalking me, calling my room and making vulgar and inappropriate suggestions. I want to know who it is!" I insisted.

"We have no way of getting that information. Have you tried the police?" he posed.

"Let me call them from here, I don't want to go back to my room." I took the phone from the bored front desk clerk and dialed the police.

The police came out and informed me that the way the off-campus dorm apartments were set up, they were completely unable to trace, track, or see what calls were coming or going. They took my statement, walked me to my door, and said good night. Nothing more. Sure, they were kind, but not very helpful in that current situation.

I knelt down beside my bed and prayed. I prayed for boldness, protection, wisdom, and whatever else I needed.

R-I-N-G.

My phone rang again. Not one to hide and shrink unless absolutely necessary, I took a few deep breaths and answered on the third ring.

"You called the police?" he rasped from the other end of the line in a whisper of betrayal.

I could hear him breathing heavily and muttering obscenities under his breath, his voice full of venom. "What do you expect? Some guy I don't know is calling me late in the evening, telling me he is watching me, and using offensive language inappropriate for any living being's ears. Of course I called the police."

"That was a big mistake," he countered. Then he began

to describe in great detail, full of vile and depraved language, what he was planning to do with me. It was lewd, horrifying, and gave me just the courage I needed to do what I did next.

I whispered a quick prayer under my breath, stood up straight and tall with my head held high, and threw open my front door. I stood there for just a moment, then yelled at the top of my lungs with fire in my eyes, "You want me? Come get me!" I paused, looking around. I waited for someone to come barrel me over, for lights to flick on, for anything to happen. The air around me felt electrified, so I continued, "I have Jesus Christ the Son of God on my side. I will not hide or cower. If you think you are so bad, then come get me here and now, in front of God and everyone, or leave me alone!"

Silence. I could hear nothing but my deep rhythmic breaths and the buzzing night insects.

I stood waiting for what felt like an eternity, and still nothing. After several minutes, I took a slow cleansing breath, turned on my heel, and walked back into my apartment surrounded with complete confidence. I shut and bolted the door with a newfound gentle calm, before having a long talk with the Lord, then finally crawling into bed for the night.

I never heard or saw any evidence from that stalker again. To my surprise, he just silently went away. Yes, I kept looking over my shoulder the rest of that semester, trying to be prepared "just in case," but that moment never came. He was gone.

To top off everything else going on during this time, Shane and I permanently parted ways as a couple. That was a difficult and trying time, but it seemed necessary. Then my best friend, who lived on the second floor of my complex, dropped out of college after being in a car accident that left him with a torn-up shoulder. I felt a bit alone and overwhelmed after being stalked and losing my closest friends so quickly, but I pushed on to finish out the semester. At the end of it all, I decided that this particular university was not for me and headed home after finals were completed. I went back to community college to finish the rest of my basics before transferring to Baylor University, in Waco, Texas.

NINE

RESTART

*Behold, I stand at the door and knock. If anyone
hears my voice and opens the door, I will come in to
him and dine with him, and he with me.*

REVELATION 3:20

(NKJV)

I transferred back to Houston Community College
(HCC) to take a breather from the insane semester I
had just endured at Texas A&M. I was going to classes,
enjoying my studies, and making new friends along the way.
After dating one person for so long and then parting ways, I
was not interested in dating again for a while. I used this
time to focus on my academics, having a pleasing life
without a stalker, or professors trying to flunk me, and
enjoying the Lord.

One thing I failed to mention earlier was that each
college semester, or summer session, God would give me a
"project." Yes, even at A&M, I had a project. A project was

a person that God would place in my path and my responsibility for the semester was to tell them about Jesus. Sure, I told a lot of people about Jesus, but the Lord made it clear that I was to make a concerted effort on the person He set before me, and He had brought one to me for each of my semesters and summer sessions thus far.

However, this semester at HCC, it seemed I might not have a project from God. I wasn't attending the local Katy HCC campus, but rather was driving to one down I-10 into Houston. I had attended the first of all my Monday/Wednesday/Friday classes on Monday. I had attended all but one of my Tuesday/Thursday classes on Tuesday, and I was walking from my tap dance elective to my final class for the semester...chemistry.

"Well, Lord, I guess you don't have a project for me this semester. It will be a nice break," I contemplated as I walked to my last class. I sat in the back of the room at one of the lab tables while the room slowly filled up with fresh-faced students. I engaged in lively conversation with Tessa, my new friend, while we waited for the professor to arrive.

One last student, a tall, skinny, and seemingly very quiet British guy, walked into the class. When I looked up and saw him for the first time, I heard, "And THAT is your project." A small groan escaped my lips after having joyfully considered the idea of not having a project this semester, but I quickly pushed away my negative thoughts.

I examined him the best I could from where I sat. He had scooped into a desk near the front of the room, opened and book, and hunkered down as if deep in study. I chuckled. "Okay, Lord. I have a project after all."

Usually these "projects" were easy to connect with. I have a fairly laid-back and easygoing personality that means making friends is not too difficult. But this particular guy posed a peculiar challenge. Chemistry was a two-hour class with the first part being a lecture, then a fifteen-minute break in the middle, and the second part labs. As our professor took roll call, I listened for this "project" student's name, and when she called "Wayne," he answered, "Here."

During break, I invited Wayne to join Tessa and me, and a few of our other classmates, to go walk the halls to stretch our legs and grab a quick snack. Wayne refused and stayed right where he was, hunched over his desk with his nose in a textbook. After a few classes of extending this same invitation and Wayne's inflexible refusal, I began to wonder what God was up to giving him to me as a project. I couldn't get more than a single word from this kid at any given time.

Finally, one day, I said, "What is your name?" knowing very well that his name was Wayne.

"John," he answered and looked back at his book.

"No, it's not. It's Wayne."

"No, it's John."

"No. It. Is. Not. It's Wayne. I hear the professor call roll at the beginning of each class. Now, you are coming with us at break today. I can't stand seeing a person sitting here in a windowless room for two hours straight and not getting up to walk around. Come on!" I demanded, with a lighthearted chuckle at the end of my otherwise forceful diatribe.

"Okay, fine," he said and schlumped along behind us around campus like a lost and confused puppy dog. Eventually, he quit following us and actually joined our merry little band.

I quickly began to realize how different Wayne was from the rest of my friends and myself. Even different from many of the other "projects" the Lord had given me in the past. While most of my friends were Christians, he was not;

thus, the reason he was a project. All my past "projects" had been non-Christians, yet we were still able to connect fairly easily and be friends. Not only was he not a Christian, but he "thought" he was a Christian because he had been raised in England and lived in the United States. He used foul language and was overall not very respectful in his speech or actions, frequently walking too closely next to me and telling me he liked my neck. That was a bit creepy. Then he would stop at every window, mirror, or other object that had a reflection to look at himself, check his hair, and preen like a peacock. I had to force myself to continue talking to him about Jesus through the semester, because if I had it my way, I would not have been hanging out with this guy. Whenever I had been around him for any length of time, I left feeling slimy like his words had drenched me in sticky goo that would not easily wash off.

The semester went on quickly, and before I knew it, it was over. Not only was it over, but I had not taken Wayne to church or had a true, deep conversation with him about the Lord. Not because I hadn't tried—I had—but he simply would not talk about issues with substance. Everything remained surface level. My friends saw me attempting to engage him in deeper soul-level talk, but after many weeks they advised me to give up after watching Wayne's eyes glaze over time and time again. I never gave up, but I had failed. We parted ways to never see each other again. Or so I thought.

Of course my family and close friends away from class knew about my Wayne project, and how I believed I had failed. Little did we know that he would be coming back into my life.

My friend Kelly and I were headed to lunch and to see a movie together one afternoon during summer break. As I drove south on Mason Road in my little blue Escort, chatting away and listening to KSBJ, I looked over my shoulder to check the blind spot on my left. Lo and behold if Wayne wasn't in the passenger's seat of the truck next to me.

"Oh no! I can't believe it!" I exclaimed.

"What?" Kelly cried.

"Don't look now, but the guy in that black truck to our left is Wayne...my failed project. I can't believe it. I didn't even know he lived around here. I assumed he lived near the campus in Houston," I stated with bewilderment in my voice.

Kelly just laughed and laughed and laughed. I think she may have even snorted once or twice. "You mean the guy who has a potty mouth and thinks you have a 'pretty neck'?" she snickered.

"Yeah, that's the one. Oh gosh, I hope he doesn't see me." I put my blinker on and pulled into the parking lot where we were headed.

"Guess what? He's following us!" Kelly chuckled.

"No way! This is so embarrassing. What should I do?"

"Roll down your window," Kelly said in a rush of words, then giggling.

So, I rolled down my window just in time for them to park next to me and for Wayne to hop out and appear at my now open window.

"Hey, um, Natalie. Um. Can I, um, have your number?" Wayne sheepishly stuttered.

"No," I declared.

Insert awkward pause here.

"Where do you work?" I finally asked, in a resigned tone. "Maybe I can stop by sometime."

"I work at Academy in the sports department," he

dejectedly answered, realizing I was giving him the brush-off.

"Okay, bye," I said and watched him climb back in the truck.

Laughter. Nothing but laughter coming from my passenger's seat. "Why didn't you give him your number?" Kelly posed.

"Because he's not a Christian. I can't just give my number to anyone."

"What are you going to do?" she queried.

"I'm going to pray and see if the Lord wants me to resume my 'project.' If He does, then I will go to Wayne's work and invite him to church," I stated matter-of-factly, but with a hint of glumness to my words. I was not ready to pick this particular project back up.

I waited a week or two, then one day I sauntered into the sporting goods department at Academy and spotted Wayne. I asked him to go to Metro with me but forgot to inform him that Metro was a college-age Bible study. Oops. He agreed, thinking it was some kind of date. I picked him up the following Monday evening and took him down to the big First Baptist Church in Houston.

To my surprise he had never been to a church before. As we approached the building, Wayne's face began to pale as he looked up at the imposing structure towering before him.

"No, no, no. I can't go in there," he whispered as he shook his head and tilted backward as if to faint.

"Oh yes you can," I asserted as I grabbed his shoulders from behind and pushed him inside. My heart was filled with a small measure of glee at making him go into church for the very first time ever.

Once inside, we gathered for worship and teaching,

meeting up with friends and enjoying the peace of the Lord. Well, at least that is what I did. Poor Wayne was squirmy and uncomfortable every moment. He very hesitantly met my friends although he was not quite able to make full eye contact with them, and was ready to bolt as soon as it was all over.

I drove him back to his home, the car as silent as a tomb with currents of tension and nerves shimmering inside the cabin. As soon as we pulled up to his driveway, Wayne jumped out of the car, leaned into the passenger side door, looked me square in the eyes and yelled, "I am never going back there again!" He slammed the door, marched into his house, and didn't even glance back.

"That went well," I muttered to myself as I drove away, and then I submitted him into the hands of God. Actually, I began a prayer tactic. Each day I included in my prayers for God to tackle and surround Wayne with Himself. I prayed for every commercial, billboard, TV show, radio station, bumper sticker, and whatever else God could use to bombard him and point him back to the Lord.

I knew that God would chase Wayne down to be His own child.

TEN

SALVATION

For I am not ashamed of the gospel, because it is the power of God that brings salvation to everyone who believes: first to the Jew, then to the Gentile.

ROMANS 1:16

(NIV)

After having a car door slammed in my face, I was fairly certain that my dealings with Wayne were over, but that was not the case. A week came and went without a single breath from him, and then on a Tuesday, the day AFTER I went to the Metro Bible study by myself, I received a phone call.

"Hello," I answered.

"Okay. So, when are we going back to that Metro thing?" a masculine voice hesitantly asked me from the other end of the phone.

"Oh. Hey, Wayne. Well, Metro was last night, but I can pick you up next week. How's that sound?" I queried with a huge smile on my face. Apparently, he knew exactly what he was doing; he needed another week to get up the nerve to go back there again.

"Um, yeah, sure. See you then," he mumbled and hung up.

I began to roar with laughter and praise the Lord for what He was up to within Wayne's heart.

I picked Wayne up that next week, and when he climbed into my car, he declared, "I can't seem to get away from this God. Every time I turn on the TV or the radio, someone is talking about Him. Even the billboards and bumper stickers have something to say about God. Everywhere. I. Look!" I giggled under my breath and simply nodded in polite acquiescence.

Each Monday after that I would pick Wayne up for the Metro Bible study. It became a ritual for us to go to Metro, then for him to come over one other day during the week to spend time in my parents' living room, asking me questions about God and the Bible.

As the summer went on, he began to think we were dating. I had to correct him and let him know that we were definitely NOT dating, and that at the end of the summer, we would part ways.

"Why? There's no reason we can't date," Wayne supposed.

"Um, YES, there is!" I exclaimed. "You are not saved, and I will only date a Christian man, to fall in love with a Christian man, and to marry a Christian man."

"Well, can't I just fake it?" he questioned.

"No, you CANNOT fake it. I can tell if you have given your heart to the Lord, and you most definitely have not. I am fully prepared to go to Baylor University, and for you to the University of Texas, and to never look back," I stated. I could see my words hurt him, but I was not willing to lead him on.

As God would have it, Wayne did accept Jesus as his Lord and Savior that summer.

On Monday, August 9, 1999, a few hours before Metro Bible study, I heard the Lord say, "Go buy Wayne a Bible. Today is the day of his salvation."

"No. I am not wasting my money on him. He will never read it. He is a lost cause," I cried to the Lord.

"Go buy him a Bible," I heard again in my spirit.

"Lord, do I really have to? I don't want to," I said in a stubborn fit.

"Natalie."

I didn't respond to the Lord after he used my name. I had every intention of disobeying Him that day but, somehow, I found myself standing at the checkout line in Rejoice Christian Bookstore with a King James Bible in my hands. King James was my favorite version, so I bought that, even if it was too difficult for most people to read and understand. My stubborn streak was coming through and I begrudgingly paid the cashier. I inscribed the Bible with these words:

Presented to: Wayne Kenneth Sherwood By: Natalie Reneé Jeu

May this gift greatly touch your life. Cherish it forever, and remember: Jesus loves you. Date: August 9, 1999 – Monday

That evening I picked Wayne up, as had become our ritual, and we drove all the way to Metro while I wrestled inside about actually giving him the Bible. Even after it was paid for and inscribed, I still struggled with giving such a gift to a person that would not appreciate it.

We pulled into the Metro parking lot. I reached into the

back seat of the car and plunked the Bible onto his lap. "Here. I got you something."

"A Bible? Oh. Okay, thanks," Wayne replied with a bewildered look on his face. He opened the front cover, read the inscription, and looked at me as though he was unsure what to do with the book.

"Bring it in with you. I'll show you where the references are during the talk," I offered.

So, in we walked to Metro Bible study, each of us carrying our own Bibles. During the talk I turned the pages of his Bible for him so he could read along. When it was over, we had a quiet drive home. God was prompting me to get really intentional and vulnerable with Wayne, and to take concerted time to give him the gospel message in story form. We had been reading the scriptures all summer. I had taught him all about what Jesus had done and why, but now God wanted me to let Himself pour from my heart.

When we arrived at Wayne's house, instead of him jumping out and me driving home, I put the car in park and turned it off. "Do you mind if I come inside and talk to you for a moment?" I requested.

"Um, sure, okay. My family might be asleep." He shrugged.

"That's fine. We can just sit on the bottom steps by the front door. There is something I want to talk with you about."

We quietly walked toward the house and sat in the entry on the stair. We were silent for what felt like an eternity, him waiting to hear what I wanted to talk about, me listening to Jesus about what to say. In a soft, dream-like voice, I began to tell Wayne the story of the scriptures we had been reading together for the past months. I started in Genesis and weaved words about how God had created man in His own image. I entreated him in the truth that we (mankind) had sinned and been separated from God, and that the penalty for that sin is death, eternal death and separation from God. I reminded him that today we are all still sinners, not one of us perfect, and all deserving of that penalty. Through the power of the Holy Spirit, I spun words together about the love of God for mankind and Him sending the perfect gift to us, a Savior in the form of a baby named Jesus, who was not only a baby and a person, but was God Himself, the Son of God, come as a man to be a perfect sacrifice to take away the penalty of sins in the world. I walked him through the life of Jesus and tears glistened in my eyes as I relayed Jesus' betrayal by friends, His scourging for our sins and diseases, His death on a Roman cross, His burial and, finally, His conquering resurrection that left death, Hell, and the grave buried behind Him in the light of His resurrected life. I declared that Jesus is ALIVE today and is calling Wayne to Himself, asking Wayne to allow Him to forgive him, wash him clean, be his God, his Lord, and his Savior.

After the long retelling of the story of the Bible, we were silent for a moment. I felt the presence of the Lord surround us, and I heard in my heart, "Tell him again."

I felt dumbfounded at the request from God to tell someone the exact same story I had just shared, but after a deep breath, I started again and retold the entire story from Creation to Salvation a second time.

Wayne began to breathe heavily, as if something was stirring inside of him, as he fingered the pages of the new Bible sitting in his lap.

The Lord's presence was thick and calming. Then I heard the Lord's voice, "Tell him the story One. More. Time."

This time I obeyed immediately, realizing that this was indeed the day of Wayne's salvation. After recounting the same story a third time, Wayne began to cry and said, "Can we pray now? Right now? I need to ask Jesus to be my God."

"Of course we can pray."

We prayed. He repented. He gave his life over to the one and only true God that is still living, willing, and able today.

"I'm floating. I'm floating," Wayne declared after we said amen. "Let's pray again. Can we pray again?"

Softly laughing, I rejoiced. "Of course we can pray again."

Again we prayed. After saying amen the second time, he begged to pray yet a third time, and so we did. He was giddy with excitement. "I feel new! This so amazing. I'm still floating. I don't think I can sleep tonight." He chuckled with the huge "Sherwood grin" plastered on his face.

I smiled at him and quietly left. As I drove home that night, I repented for my stubborn disobedience earlier in the day and rejoiced in the new soul I would get to spend eternity with.

Wayne changed immediately. He no longer had a potty mouth. He began to shine with the love of the Lord and he started getting divine revelation about what in the world was truth and what was not. This was all the work of the Holy Spirit within him, as I never had to tell him to stop using curse words.

Not too long after that, we begin dating, for now he was a man I might actually consider for marriage.

ELEVEN

CHANGE

I have told you these things, so that in me you may have peace. In this world you will have trouble. But take heart! I have overcome the world.

JOHN 16:33
(NIV)

The summer ended and Wayne and I began a long-ish-distance relationship as he went off to the University of Texas, in Austin, and I traipsed off to Baylor, in Waco. When I first started college, my initial thought was to get a microbiology degree and a nursing degree to fall back on, but that was not going to happen. Since my dad was paying for my schooling, he required me to change my degree to business with the promise that I could change back next semester if I absolutely hated it.

Looking back, I wish I had pushed harder and kept my science degree plan because I did indeed hate business, and fully intended to switch back next semester.

Back when I had enrolled at Texas A&M, I was told I had to have the hepatitis B vaccination by my junior year of college to remain on the microbiology program plan I had chosen. The hepatitis B vaccination is a series of three shots over approximately six months. I had scheduled to get these shots with my doctor when I was home from A&M during the summer that had just ended. I received my last shot just before heading off to Baylor.

"Yes!" I thought. "It is finished! No more vaccinations and I can move ahead." That third shot felt different that the first two though. It hurt a lot and my arm and shoulder were sore for several days. No big deal though, that is a common side effect.

I packed my car and moved off to a city that was about a three-hour drive from my family home. I moved into an apartment with my new roommate, Carrie, and walked the route to my classes so I would be ready for the first day. I skipped around and allowed myself to simply get excited for the semester ahead.

My new home had a peaceful feel to it. The campus was full of large oak trees that were a vibrant green and gave cooling shade on those hot Texas days. The students had smiles on their faces, and new friends seemed to find each other easily.

After my personal unpleasant experience at Texas A&M, I looked forward to having a fellow Christian as a roommate. We each had our own bedroom and bathroom, and a shared living room, kitchen, breakfast, and laundry area. We had our own space but could also come together to enjoy each other's company.

Sonny was Carrie's yellow, white, and gray cockatiel. He was allowed out of his cage when we were home, and he would talk to us by whistling and copying the noises we made. I happen to be a hot tea drinker, which made for great entertainment with that bird. I would put the kettle on, and when it would whistle, Sonny would bob his head up and down looking for the other bird. He would groom his feathers, dance, and strut his stuff trying to win that hot and smoky kettle of a girl bird. It was the funniest thing; too bad for him it was only a teakettle.

Classes started without a hitch, and I made some good friends. Carrie and her cockatiel bird were the best. I couldn't have asked for a better, more like-minded roomie. As it was Carrie's final year at the university, our class schedules were quite different, so we didn't see each other all that much, but once a week we tried to eat dinner together while watching her favorite sitcom instead of just saying "hi" and "bye" in passing. We were both pretty laid-back and she was easy to get along with.

Often, while I was studying alone in my room, I would hear her take out her violin to practice. Her music was calming, and her spirit was beautiful. The notes would rise off her instrument like waves crescendoing off the ocean floor, bringing with it a sense of relaxation and joy. Of course, it didn't hurt that the violin was my absolute favorite instrument to listen to either.

In my business classes I was assigned a team of three guys to write a semester business plan with where we had to start our own business and "pitch" it to investors. This team of guys and I meshed really well, and we became great friends for the short time we worked together. All four of us were Christians and had very strong faith and convictions. I learned that is a bonus of going to a Christian University; most of your friends are already fairly like-minded. Oh, don't get me wrong, the party scene and wild life still existed for some, but not for any of the people that I grew close to, or myself. The four of us "business partners" stayed up many late nights writing, planning, and eating fast food; well, they ate fast food and I ate the salad. So many times I wondered if I would get to bed before it was time to wake up, but in the end it seemed so worth it to study together and build this camaraderie.

One afternoon, I pulled into the parking lot to find my roommate and several friends walking around the grounds whistling and clicking their tongues.

"Whistle, whistle. Smooch, smooch, smooch," I heard as I exited my car.

"What's going on? Why are you doing that?" I queried. I wanted to laugh at how absurd everyone looked, leaning down and peering under bushes or calling up into trees with kissing and whistling noises, but once I realized what had happened—Sonny the cockatiel had escaped and flown out of our apartment—I joined in.

"Sonny, where are you? Come here, Sonny. Come home. Here, boy, here." We whistled, hunted, prayed, and called as if he was a lost dog. Our apartment was near the highway, and several flocks of birds flew by during our search. We were so afraid that Sonny had either been run over or had simply flown away with some new friends. We continued to pray and search, and you know what? Sonny was brought home safe that day. That silly bird came strutting up to us like nothing was wrong. He had just been out for a little stroll. From then on, we were extra careful to keep Sonny in his house unless we were sure that no one was coming in or going out.

I went to classes during the week and studied hard, or simply cried over my textbooks. Wayne would come visit on many of the weekends. Mostly he did the driving to visit

Waco, but on occasion I would go stay with some of his friends in the girls' dorm down in Austin.

Baylor had a live bear that we would go visit, then we would sit in the beautiful courtyard dotted with trees and just talk about the Lord. We spent many weekend afternoons lounging under the deep green leaves watching the puffy white clouds float by in the endless blue Texan sky. It was so still and peaceful that we could hear the Lord's voice on the whisper of the wind. We often found ourselves singing worship songs out of the overflow of His goodness. It was so very refreshing, until it was time to study again.

Wayne witnessed my utter failure and distaste for learning all things business that semester. What was I thinking changing my major? Seriously? I loved the sciences, I was good at the sciences, and I got the needed vaccinations to continue the sciences. Nonetheless, as Dad was paying the tuition, the major changed to business. Sure, I can understand daily business just fine, but the textbook learning of such methods and ideas was gibberish to me. I truly don't know how I got the grades I did except for the grace of God, and that does not mean that the grades were good!

Not only were the business classes nonsense to me, but something else unseen was also going on. Something inside my body was stirring up trouble and waiting to pounce.

What came next was a comedy of errors, or maybe it would be better stated as the perfect storm. What could go wrong did go wrong. Looking back, I am so grateful that God decided to build my faith so heavily in my younger caterpillar years or I would not have made it through this upcoming trial with the grace I did.

TWELVE

IT BEGINS

*Praise be to the God and Father of our Lord Jesus
Christ, the Father of compassion and the God of all
comfort, who comforts us in all our troubles, so that
we can comfort those in any trouble with the comfort
we ourselves receive from God.*

2 CORINTHIANS 1:3-4

(NIV)

Have you ever stopped to ponder your biggest fears? Oh sure, we are afraid of some everyday things, but those are superficial fears; surface level. Like my aversion to spiders or my extreme dislike of heights. Those are obvious fears; they don't dig deep and change my life. They are more annoyances than anything. I used to run away screaming from spiders...not so much anymore. I still avoid heights but can fly on an airplane or drive on an overpass if I need to. Coming face to face with a spider will most likely cause me varying degrees of discomfort based on the spider's size, but I don't have some sort of internal life transformation every time I see one. I don't have a "coming to Jesus" moment each time I am forced to cross over a high bridge. I pray for safety and breathe a little deeper, but I don't come down on the other side of the bridge transformed into a different person. The fears I am talking about are bigger than you; gripping and life-changing fears.

If someone had asked me what my biggest fears were as a child, I could have easily told them what they were. I knew them. I did not live with them, I was never troubled or anxious that they would actually happen, I just knew deep down that those were the things that would strike fear into me.

When you dig deep into yourself, what would truly strike fear into you? Being laughed at for your failures? Being caught in a sin? Not being able to provide or not being provided for? Illness? Not living? Maybe a fear of dying?

I wasn't afraid of dying. I knew God and knew where I would go. Provision didn't bother me either. I had always been provided for. As you can probably imagine from the few stories I told you previously, even in the very hard financial times, God showed up. I wasn't living with some egregious sin that would rip me apart once discovered either. No. My biggest fears were things that most people probably don't even give a second thought. My fears were of being paralyzed, going blind, or being trapped in a body full of pain in a hospital with nothing I could do about it, all while having to remain alive. It wasn't the dying that was scary; it was the existing through illness or pain that seemed so foreboding.

As unfounded as they were, these were my fears. When I saw one of those things in a movie, I would cringe inside wondering how a person made it through, but I never expected they would actually happen to me. I simply did not think about them. They didn't cause me anxiety or panic, but I knew they were there in the back of my mind. I knew if I was asked about them, that I could list them. Little did I know that I was about to face them, all of them.

So begins a new stage. I am a fat and happy caterpillar, enjoying the lazy "eating" days of my life. I still live in a deep daily relationship with my Lord. He is still showing up as the still small voice day after day in my life, but something is changing. I don't know it yet, but I am being wrapped in my cocoon.

About thirty days after my final hepatitis B vaccination, while living at Baylor, I got the flu. I had never had the flu before. Oh sure, I got sick growing up. I suffered with allergies, headaches, ear infections, bronchitis, strep throat, and stomachaches, but those would come and go, lasting a relatively short amount of time when they did strike. Those illnesses were yucky but weren't all too bad by and large. But this flu hit me hard. I was away at college and basically crawled to my lectures to sit in the very back chair in the room, then crawled back to my apartment. For about ten days, I locked myself in my room, drank water, and slept between my classes. I couldn't go out, couldn't go to the gym, couldn't study and didn't even want to talk on the phone. I forbade my boyfriend from coming to visit because I didn't want him to catch whatever I had. Little did I know that what I had was only the beginning of a chain reaction within.

After ten days, I felt better. Well, seemingly better. I never did fully recover from that virus. I was still tired and felt off, but I was no longer sick.

I regained my social life, fell back into my healthy

workout and eating routine, and dug into studying. I stayed up late, poring over those mind-numbingly boring business textbooks to make sure my grades didn't suffer.

Then I became ill again, and again. Every thirty days I would fall back into a mild flu-like illness. None of them were as bad as the initial flu, but the achiness, exhaustion, and headaches would return for a few days, go away, then come back one month later. This repetitive cycle continued the rest of that semester and frazzled my nerves.

Somehow, I passed my classes with decent grades, hugged my friends' necks, packed up my car and headed back home for summer break. I was worn down from the hard semester and recurring illness. Now nineteen years old and halfway through my junior year of college, I was ready to relax some. I was really looking forward to my first summer since graduating high school where I could simply reconnect with old friends and not take any classes.

I also decided to begin treatment to help with the temporomandibular joint syndrome (TMJ) I had that was caused by wearing braces as a pre-teen. It was no big deal, but every dentist I had ever gone to remarked on the extreme popping my jaw would do and thought it would be best if I could get it treated. It just so happened that a family friend had been going through treatment for her TMJ and was having great success, so she referred me to her dentist and I started my treatments. After all, I wasn't taking classes that summer, so this would be an easy time to have my jaw all fixed up.

I spent the first few weeks of summer connecting with old friends, catching up on lost sleep, having fun and wearing my new TMJ mouthpieces. Everything seemed to be fine until one morning, about thirty days after my last flu-like illness, I was suddenly slammed with a migraine. I had experienced pretty bad headaches off and on through life, but this was something altogether different. I couldn't tolerate sound of any kind or even the tiniest bit of light.

I had a lovely bedroom with two large windows and an en suite bath. This was great when I felt good, but with this migraine, the light from those windows was torture. Nothing my parents or I did seemed to block out the light enough. My parents even went so far as to nail quilts over my bedroom windows in an attempt to block the light out completely. I didn't connect the migraine to the flu-like illnesses I had suffered through during my last semester because I was past that, and this was NOT the same.

My first reaction was to run to the dentist that was heading up my TMJ treatments. I thought the movement of my jaw was causing the pain, and when I went to the appointment, the dentist concurred. He noted that the treatment could indeed cause severe headaches that would last a few days, but that they should subside as my body settled into its new normal. He also verified that my jaw had indeed moved considerably and that I was ready for the next mouthpiece. So, he fitted me with the next retainer, wrote me a few days prescription for codeine, and sent me on my way.

After a few days of wearing my new retainer, taking the codeine, and staying curled up on my rose-patterned bedspread, I thought I should be much better, but I was worse. The pain never let up and was spreading down to my neck and shoulders. I couldn't think, couldn't eat, and thought my head was going to explode.

The slightest movement sent me reeling and collapsing in a heap of tortured limbs. I hadn't had a moment of rest for days, so I took out the mouthpiece. My jaw was not relaxing, my body was not settling into its new normal, and

I needed relief. Removing the mouthpiece, which I assumed would bring respite, did nothing. The codeine did nothing. I just kept getting worse. I didn't even think there could be a worse, but somehow worse still came.

My mom and I went back to the dentist after office hours so the workplace would be quiet, and the doctor could have most of the lights turned off for me. I actually had to ride in the car with my eyes covered by a towel because the dim of twilight hurt so much. Not only that, but the sway and motion of the car had me wanting to retch, but I hadn't eaten, so that was not possible.

This visit to the dentist was exceedingly emotional. He was confounded as to why I was experiencing this pain. This had never happened before in his practice. My mom was beside herself with worry and I was simply unable to function, just lying in the dental chair moaning in the dark. What had happened? Could TMJ treatments really be to blame for a fun, healthy, vibrant nineteen-year-old girl completely collapsing into her room of solitude and dark-ness? We ended the TMJ treatments that day, but the pain continued on.

The next day we were able to get into an emergency appointment to see my regular family physician. I was ushered in, checked out, and diagnosed with migraines. Okay, really? Is that all? I now suffer from migraines? I thought migraines came on, lasted one to three days, then went away to come back another day. This migraine had been slamming my head for much longer, without having let up even for a moment. But that was the diagnosis, so what was the treatment?

The doctors were so very calm, and lovingly assured me that they were going to give me a shot for the pain. This shot would also put me to sleep for the next several hours. I was told that it should knock out the migraine and then we would move forward from there. Wonderful! That was music to my ears. I would feel no pain and my sleep-deprived body would get some relief. "Hurry up! Get me that shot!" I thought.

I lay back on the exam table with the lights off in the room. The nurse came in and administered the shot. I closed my eyes, hoping and waiting for it to take effect, and it did. I have no idea what they gave me, but the pain started to ebb ever so slightly. Mostly, the drug just started to put me to sleep with much of the pain still intact.

Oh no! I felt trapped in a twilight zone with a powerful pain in my head and a body that acted asleep. My eyes were closed, my body was still, but I could still hear my mom and the doctor and nurses. After a few minutes, everyone except my mom left the room and I just lay there in the darkness. I knew they thought I was asleep because I had heard them talking about me, but I was not asleep. I knew they thought I was pain-free, but I was not pain-free. My greatest fear had come true; I was trapped. I kept thinking that I did not want to be trapped in a sleeplike state for the next several hours. I wanted to sleep, for real, not pretend. I wanted to feel no pain, but that was not to be so.

After only fifteen minutes of receiving the shot, I suddenly woke completely up and bolted to an upright sitting position.

It surprised my mom and the physician's assistant who had peeked her head back into the room to check on us. They were sure I would be out for hours. But there I was, sitting on the end of the exam table, wide-awake and in agony. I didn't have the heart to say anything. My body was not fully responsive yet as the medication still needed to wear off, so we stayed awhile longer before grabbing a prescription for migraines and heading home. My mom had to practically carry me to the car because the medication had my body feeling heavy and limp. We would return to the doctor if things didn't improve over the next few days.

I didn't know, but my cocoon had been spun.

After a few days of no response to the migraine medication, I suddenly started vomiting. We had been told that migraines could cause nausea, but I hadn't been eating. My mom was trying to coax food into me in tiny spoonfuls but my stomach rejected everything. I retched violently anytime I took food or liquid into my body. I could hold nothing down. I was exhausted, weak, full of pain, and lonely.

Wayne knew I had been sick, so he spent his time moving back home from college for his summer break and began working his summer job. He had no idea of the craziness that was going on because everything had happened so fast, but he would soon find out.

THIRTEEN

PARALYZED

*For God hath not given us the spirit of fear; but of
power, and of love, and of a sound mind.*

2 TIMOTHY 1:7
(KJV)

My life was about to change today and it would be so
much worse than a migraine. My cocoon had been
spun and was way too small. What was happening to my fat
caterpillar body?

I have always been an early riser. I often woke up
around 4:45 a.m. I had been doing this for years. This habit
was established in junior high when the homework load was
too much for me to complete in the evenings. I would wake
up to finish what I could, then get ready and go off to school.
Then, in high school, I became involved in sports and cheerleading, so the mornings were when I would do much of my
review work and also spend alone time with the Lord.

I would wake up, pray, take a shower, slowly dry my

hair, fix my morning cup of hot tea, and watch the sunrise. I loved my quiet mornings talking to God and watching the sky change from dark and starry to bright and new. I never tired of it. I have watched a thousand silent sunrises and each one still looked beautiful and fresh, signaling a chance to start all over.

I especially loved the change in sound. While it was still dark, I could hear the chorus of crickets and frogs, but as the sky's light began to change, the insects would find their beds and quiet down at the same time the birds would begin to wake up and sing. The smell of daybreak is so refreshing. It is clean and new, and it sets your mind straight. Watching, hearing, and smelling the beginning of a new day is calming and stimulating. It prepared me for what was to come, especially when I was able to spend many of those mornings with my parents. Those quiet relationship-building moments. No talking needed, just silently enjoying creation waking up for another dawn.

This particular Saturday morning I stayed in my room. Even with the migraines I would wander into the dark kitchen in the mornings at 4:45 a.m. for a change of scenery. Getting out of bed and walking around before it was too bright for me to be in any room other than my bedroom with its covered windows. But not this day. No, this day I stayed in my room. Not because I wanted to, but because I had to. Yes, my cocoon was stifling.

I opened my eyes at 4:45 a.m. No alarm clock was ever needed. My body was used to this time and simply woke up on its own. I opened my eyes and looked at my clock, its green numbers facing me from my nightstand. Normally, I swung my legs over the side of my bed and used my arms to push up, but nothing happened. I didn't move. I couldn't move. "Am I still asleep? Here, let me try again," I thought.

Nothing. "Maybe I can reach over and turn on my clock radio." Nothing.

My arms and legs would not respond. "Okay, I know, I'll just roll over, then push myself up off the floor. Roll. Roll. Come on, roll over." Nothing. "I can't move." The realization started to sink in.

"No, wait. I'm really asleep. I'm dreaming and I'll wake up any moment, jump out of bed and I'll be fine. This must be that moment just before I wake up, but I only think I am awake...like twilight. Right?"

For the next few hours, I tried over and over again to throw off my blankets or kick my feet off the side of my bed. Since I couldn't move or roll over, I was forced to watch the clock glare at me, each green number mocking my inability to climb out of bed. Each minute felt like an hour of its own. I kept saying to myself, "Okay, this time." Then I would try with all my might to get up, yet nothing would happen.

"Okay, this time.

Okay, this time.

This time!"

My body wilted, as it lay there immobile.

I was somehow very calm; I can only attribute that to God. I was even kind to myself. I would very politely tell myself, "Don't worry because this time it will work, and you will get up." Or I would try to psych myself out like I used to do for the sports teams back in my cheerleading days. "Come on, you can do it this time!"

Do you know what happens to a caterpillar's mind when her cocoon seals shut? Realization sets in. She realizes that she is in a dark, lonely, confined, and sometimes painful place. She begins to wonder how long she can last like this. Fear tries to reach out its long, spindly fingers to take hold. I wouldn't allow it. Fear would have no place here! I didn't know what was happening, but I could fight this. With God I could fight this.

Despite my inability to move, I stayed optimistic. I didn't panic and I kept praying in my mind. "Wake up, move. Anything! Move hands! Move arms, feet, legs. Just move." Zero. Zilch. Nada. My body wouldn't produce even a wiggle of a movement.

My parents usually woke up around 6 a.m., so I knew they would come check on me if I wasn't wandering around the kitchen. Nope, not today.

I watched the clock while 6 a.m. came and went. "An hour and fifteen minutes have already passed." I listened as my dad got ready and went to work. He didn't check on me.

I watched as the clock turned to 7 a.m. "I've been lying here over two hours." I listened as my mom puttered around in the kitchen.

I screamed and yelled for her: "Help! Mom! Please, somebody help me. Can you hear me? Help!" But my vocal cords were useless. My loudest scream produced the softest whisper. And screaming was so tiring. I could only try it about once every five to ten minutes, and even that seemed to steal too much of my body's limited energy.

I had been throwing my whole strength and energy into trying to get out of bed, or screaming for help, for over five hours when my mom finally peeked her head around the L-shaped wall that divided my bedroom door from the hallway. I always left my door open. It was just past 10 a.m.

Unknown to me, my mom had been checking on me. She had been coming up to my door, but when she couldn't hear me, she thought I was finally sleeping. She didn't dare wake me. Not after days of migraine pain and sleepless nights. She was being loving and letting me sleep. Only I wasn't asleep, I was trapped. The only thing that seemed to be working was my mind. My mind was sharp and clear, and the migraine was gone. Actually, I had no pain anywhere. No pain, just...what? What was I? Paralyzed!

My mom finally came all the way into my room. When I caught sight of her in my peripheral vision, I mustered all the strength I had and yelled as loud as I could in a soft scratchy voice, "I can't move." I thought she wouldn't hear me. After all, I had been screaming for hours and I could barely hear myself. I couldn't turn my head to look at her or move to signal her. I just had to yell and hope.

She heard me. Yes, she heard me all right. "What!" she shrieked. She jumped about a foot in the air while screaming and lunging toward me. Then she frantically yelled, "What do you mean?" She grabbed me by the shoulders, flung my legs over the side of the bed and yanked me up to a sitting position, pulling me tight up against her. She knew immediately. Her mother's intuition kicked in and she knew that I was unable to move.

Yes, this cocoon was strange. Not anything like the life of eating, growing, and shedding I had experienced. This was different. I was changing.

After taking care of me and getting me settled on the sofa (there was no way she was leaving me in my room alone), my mom called the doctor. This was an emergency.

Have you ever been sick on the weekend? Doctors are hard to reach. Nowadays they have urgent care rooms, but back then it was your doctor or the nearest emergency room (ER). Since I had been under my doctor's care for the migraine headaches, we tried her first. She was not on duty that Saturday, but the doctor "on call" would see me immediately.

My mom had notified my dad, so he had gone to get me a wheelchair and came home with the most uncomfortable, stiff, and rickety chair he could find. The thing looked like scrap metal he found at a junkyard with a piece of pleather fabric strapped to it to act as a seat.

"I am not going to buy you a wheelchair," he told me with a look on his face like he had a big joke brewing in his mind. "I rented the worst one I could find because you won't be staying in it. You will be walking soon."

"Okay, Dad, good message. I get it. I can jump on board with that, but for now can you just put me in the wheelchair and push me to the car?" I resorted to thinking my responses instead of speaking them. It hurt to talk, and I was not easily understood with this new whispered, scratchy squeak of mine.

I didn't have to wait too long for the doctor on call but, honestly, at this time in my life, everything seemed like an eternity. My senses had slowly heightened as the day wore on, and they were beyond anything I had ever experienced before. I could hear the ticking of every clock and watch in that waiting room. And with each second that ticked by, I felt a little more life leaving my body.

Once called into an exam room, I was wheeled back to see the doctor. He checked me out while I sat in my wheelchair. He looked at my now drooping face, shone a bright light into my eyes and watched as my pupils dilated and contracted. He listened to my heart, my breathing, and my gut. He walked around me, eying me as if I was a stone sculpture, and that was it. My exam was over.

He completed what felt like a baby's wellness check, not a thorough examination. I was never asked to stand up or lie down. He never even touched me to check my organs or reflexes or anything else. No balance test, no breathing or speaking test, and absolutely no blood work, electrocardiogram (EKG), electroencephalogram (EEG), spinal tap, computerized axial tomography scan (CAT Scan) or other test that could possibly look into the situation; look into me.

He did listen to our story thus far. As he listened to my mom relay the TMJ treatments and the migraine headaches, he plastered on his professional white-toothed grin and looked down at me like a real-life Cheshire cat. Something felt wrong. Off. Was he really listening? Did he see enough to know what was wrong? According to the smug look on his face, his nodding "bobblehead," and the haughty attitude that kept him standing the entire time, I'm not even sure he was listening. After my mom finished the current telling of my story, I expected a frenzy of activity. I envisioned him sending me off for CAT scans and MRIs while attempting to place an IV into my dehydrated veins.

"Nothing is wrong with you," he very calmly stated.

"What?!?!?!?!" I wanted to get up and yell in his face, but instead I just yelled inside of my head. Too bad my facial expressions were unable to change due to this new drooping thing. He could have read a few choice thoughts passing across it in fleeting little moments of outrage and pain. "NOTHING WRONG? Are you crazy? Do you see me? Are you even looking? Hello! How did I go from working out, eating healthy, running five to ten miles daily, filled with life and enthusiasm, to migraines and paralysis in a matter of weeks? Come on, just order a blood test. Or better yet, send me to a neurologist." That last word "neurologist" actually made its way out of my mouth as a frog's whisper.

"A neurologist? Why would I do that? That would cost a lot of time and money for your family that they do not need to spend. You are having anxiety attacks from the migraines, and the anxiety has caused Bell's palsy," stated the doctor matter-of-factly.

"Huh? Oh no you don't! Don't explain what Bell's palsy is to me. I know what Bell's palsy is. You are crazy." I tried and tried to tell him that I didn't have anxiety and that I did not have Bell's palsy, but with my whispered, shaky, croaking squeaks there was no convincing him. He couldn't even tell I was trying to talk and just spoke over me.

He smiled his million-dollar smile, handed me a ten-day steroid packet, and said I would be better in a week.

I mustered all the strength and determination I had and yelled, "I want a referral to a neurologist."

"No," he refused. He convinced my family that a referral would be a waste of time and money because the steroids would take care of everything. He also advised us that I was now under his care, not my usual physician's care, and that I should call him for anything I needed, but to not call before ten days had elapsed because the steroids would take care of everything.

That was a load of wishful thinking, huh?

I went home.

I went home with what felt like a death sentence.

I went home and started my steroid pack.

I started my steroid pack and by that night I was not only paralyzed, but even more strange things began happening in my body.

Was I forming my wings?

FOURTEEN

ALL DOWN HILL

*For our light affliction, which is but for a moment,
worketh for us a far more exceeding and eternal
weight of glory; while we look not at the things which
are seen, but at the things which are not seen: for the
things which are seen are temporal; but the things
which are not seen are eternal.*

2 CORINTHIANS 4:17-18
(KJV)

I was desperate to get better this first night of my
paralysis. I had to figure out the source of the problem. I
was also fixated on making my body respond, cooperate. I
was able to stand by supporting my weight on my own legs
for a minute or two at a time, but only if someone had
pulled me up into the standing position and balanced me
like a block on a strong foundation.

Although I was "paralyzed," I could feel everything,
and so much more than everything. My senses had become

super heightened. The smallest whisper of a breeze on my skin made me feel like I was being skinned alive. The lightest brush of someone else's skin against mine was excruciating and electrifying. Lights were brighter, shadows were deeper, and sounds penetrated into my head like a cacophony of noise instead of their usual intended purpose.

If someone did assist me to a standing position, they had to have a firm grip on me and not slide or glide their hands along my skin. This sliding motion made the nerves in my entire body fire like lightning, and then the nerves would all short out as if they had been fried, leaving me in a heap of pain and confusion. Once I was in a standing position, which I demanded to be placed in over and over again so I could conquer this thing that had taken over my body, that was all I could do: stand. Oh, and not even standing up straight and tall either. Nope, my body was hunched and withered with no strength. I couldn't even hold my head up to look someone in the eye. My gaze was aimed at the floor, not out of choice, but simply because my head and neck muscles were too weak and unresponsive.

My arms and legs would not obey my commands either, so walking was out of the question. That first night I was persistent and made my dad pull me to a standing position over and over again because I was going to walk.

"I can walk. I know I can. I've been walking my whole life. Daddy, can you help me? Please?" I whined in my whispered croak.

Without a word he wrapped his arms under my armpits and began taking slow, deliberate steps. I sort of wiggled from side to side like a worm, trying to throw one leg in front of the other. My legs did not move and instead I just made it more difficult for Daddy to hold my already dead weight; kind of like trying to carry a greased piglet around on its hind legs.

As I wiggled in his capable arms, he hauled me around in circles skirting our large living room. "I can't do this," he stated after that first lap around the room. "I need to stop. Why don't you lie down?" he croaked, with a voice trying not to break with unshed tears.

"No, I am not sitting down or lying down. Please. Let's try again," I said. "Of course I can walk. I have been walking my whole life," I thought.

His soft, warm hands wrapped around me were comforting. The firm steps of his strong legs gave me courage. I needed my daddy and pulled on his strength to get through that first night.

Up. Drag. Sit. Up. Drag. Sit. We did this for hours while praying and praying and praying. Finally, there came a point when my daddy could not drag me around anymore. It was backbreaking, heartbreaking, and possibly even faith shattering.

I took my steroid and lived each day worse off than the day before. All the while new and strange sensations began to assault my body.

It had been a few weeks since the first onset of symptoms that I correlated as beginning with the migraine headaches, and only a day since the complete paralysis, but anyone who has experienced a sudden tragedy in their life knows that time loses all meaning. It could have been mere minutes or years since all of this began. I no longer had a sense of time, days or even hours. Each minute seemed to stretch on into eternity. Each day was endless and I would find myself longing for night, only to be worse off during the dark hours and begging for day again.

I was exhausted. I hadn't slept since the first onset of

migraine headaches. Oh, I tried to sleep, I craved sleep and would have done just about anything to fall asleep, but my body was in such a constant state of pain and turmoil that it simply would not rest.

The only "sleep" I actually obtained was when my body decided it had endured enough and would literally shut down. I would essentially pass out for fifteen to twenty minutes at a time, only to awaken with pain that was such a stark contrast from passed-out nothingness that it would bolt me upright, then throw me down again into complete helplessness.

I have heard that enemy camps often use sleep deprivation as a tool of war, and I fully understand why. It can drive a person insane. Eyes so heavy with fatigue they feel as if they will certainly never open again if closed. A brain so full of fog, and a body so heavy and full of pain, that the one being tortured wishes for death. I often wondered how I was even alive without the sleep I so frantically yearned for.

It was not only the lack of sleep—the pain and new sensations were overwhelming.

The migraines were gone, thank you, Jesus, but each time the air-conditioning turned on and blew over my skin, I felt like how I imagined a fish would feel being skinned alive. I also began having strange and horrible pins-and-needles sensations in my hands, feet, and face. Have you ever sat on your foot too long that it fell asleep, then when you moved or tried to get up, you experienced a painful pins-and-needles feeling rushing to the area trying to return blood flow? That is what this felt like in my hands, feet, and face all the time. And it wasn't just a light forbearance of pain and sensations, it was powerful and devastating, coming in typhoon-sized ocean waves.

On top of losing my voice, the being-skinned-alive pain,

and now the pins-and-needles sensations, I began to experience double and triple vision that made it difficult to look at any one object for more than a few seconds. My eyes also ceased blinking at proper intervals on their own which dried them out, and of course my brain couldn't tell my eyes to blink when I asked it to. This drying made the double and triple objects blurry and wavy, almost as if stationary items were moving in a mirage-like fashion. Looking around would greatly upset my stomach and keep me on the precipice of severe nausea. I continually felt like I was on a roller coaster that had escaped from its tracks and was catapulting through the air.

If this wasn't bad enough, I began to have muscle spasms. In the south we like to call those charley horses. You know those exceedingly agonizing foot cramps you get after running too far or not drinking enough water? The ones that can wake you from a dead sleep and make you plummet to the floor screaming? Yeah, those! I started getting those, but not in my feet. My feet already had that crazy pins-and-needles thing going on. Nope, I got these extra-special charley horses in my calves, arms, and even my face!

Is that even possible?

I am here to tell you that yes, it is possible to get facial charley horses, and it is horrible. One muscle would charley horse, stay tight for a few minutes of excruciating pain, and then release. Then the next muscle would do this too, and it would rotate around my body nonstop day and night. There was no relief, no rest from the constant input of stimulus and sensations running through my body. It was like my body was hooked up to an electrical outlet with a continual current that had no place to go.

My mom was my cheerleader during this time. She even

went to buy me a fuzzy green blanket, combing store shelves to find just the right one for me. Why? Because one day she asked me, "Natalie, what could help make you feel better? Can you think of anything?"

"A soft, fuzzy green blanket," was my odd reply. So, she scoured the stores and came home with exactly the green blanket my imagination had conjured up. And, yes, that forest green color and soft material helped to soothe me when I needed it most.

Together my mom and I lost sleep, lost complete track of time, and lost a bit of our sanity. I began "sleeping" in bed with her while my dad slept in my bed across the other side of the house. Well, to be more accurate, my mom and I began coexisting in the same bed during the dark hours of day. Nights were always worse. There were no distractions to help divert the pain, and each sensation was heightened to unparalleled precedence.

The charley horses were longer and stronger in the quiet dark hours, and each night, in the hush of my mind, I begged the Lord to let me die. Whenever a groan inadvertently escaped my lips, my mom would jump up from her light sleep next to me and begin to massage my calf muscles to help make the spasms stop. She had to massage with a vise grip because light touches hurt me so badly. She would knead and massage my muscles as if her own life depended on it, until she thought I was asleep or passed out, then she would lie down next to me and pass out herself.

After several nights of this, Mommy began hearing phantom groans coming from my side of the bed. She would jump up from her sleep to rub cramps that I was not having. Kind of like a new mother hearing their newborn baby crying in the night only to check on them and find that it was a dream. It was a living nightmare, yet the doctor said not to contact him for ten days...so we continued on.

Somehow, I still had most of my mind. My mind was sharp and clear and always thinking and praying. I wanted answers. I talked to God, I leaned on my mom, but I honestly didn't think about anyone else at this early stage of my illness. Not my friends, not my boyfriend, not my schooling, job, wants, dreams, or desires. Nothing else existed in this universe of pain and delirium.

"God, heal me. What is this? How long will this last? Will I get better? Will I die? How long do I have to live like this? God, help!" The thoughts that constantly barraged my mind seemed to carry on the wind without an echo of an answer.

Since I had lost my voice, it was very difficult to communicate to others around me. My mom learned to understand my high-pitched, whispered, croaking sounds as words, similar to how a mother learns to understand her toddler's first babbling words. Everyone else only caught glimpses of what I would try to say, and that was if I spoke at all. It was so difficult and exhausting to speak that I mostly kept my thoughts to myself. The only real sounds coming from me were groans of pain that I didn't even know I made until someone asked me what was wrong.

Yes, this cocoon was tight, and it was starting to get dark.

During this ten-day waiting period, I was diligent in taking the prescribed steroid pack. "You know these things won't work...right? Steroids are not going to fix what is wrong with me," I squeaked as Mommy handed me my next dose.

"I don't know what else to do. You have to take them,"

she pleaded exhaustedly. "Let's just try to keep these down. Okay?"

I say "taking" the steroid pack lightly because getting them down me was a chore. My body was rejecting food and liquid of any kind. Frankly, I was starving to death faster than the illness was killing me. I learned that if I just took a tiny sip of water and swallowed the pill, it would stay down, but it gave me a stomachache because I never had any other food or liquid in it.

I tried sundry soups that came back up violently after just a few sips from a spoon. I tried different fruits since they were also full of hydration, but they were watery enough that they would come back up with volcanic force and shoot out my nose, burning my sinus cavities. Once I even had fruit juice come out with such extreme power that it shot out my tear ducts. Hey, not everyone can claim that accomplishment! That must be some kind of Guinness World Record.

It got to where I would sit in my uncomfortable jalopy of a rented wheelchair, in the dark silence, with a large Tupperware bowl in my lap before taking any medicine or while trying a new food. That way, when it all came back up, I had a bowl to catch it in. Due to the paralysis, I was unable to run to the bathroom, so cleanup became remarkably difficult.

Some of the foods burned worse than you can imagine on the way up, so one day we got the bright idea to try peanut butter since it is smooth, creamy, and full of protein. What could go wrong with that? It certainly wouldn't burn making an extreme exit.

WARNING: DO NOT EAT PEANUT BUTTER if you think you might be sick. Trust me on this one. It is sticky and becomes lodged in your throat on the way back up so you think you will suffocate to death before anything else has a chance to kill you.

After a near-death experience, peanut butter and I had an unstable relationship going forward. Actually, I divorced peanut butter in a long and bitter battle. I won the house and the cars though. It took years before I could even stand the smell, let alone the taste of peanut butter again.

I did, however, find one food that I could hold down in limited quantities: oranges. Oranges became my new best friend, and unlike my former relationship with peanut butter, oranges and I fell in love. Well, that's not exactly true. It was more of a necessary, tolerant relationship.

At first, I was so excited that one orange segment stayed down that I had visions of eating an entire orange in one sitting. Maybe even an entire orange tree. It turned out my limit was two orange segments at a time. Goodbye orange tree, it was nice dreaming of you. But, honestly, after a few weeks of not eating anything, the oranges were a Godsend. And I could eat them with my snake oil steroid pack pills.

That was the good news. The bad news was that after eating I would get a strong metallic taste in my mouth, so I wanted to brush my teeth every few hours during the day. Right...brush my teeth with hands that didn't work.

Again, my mom came to the rescue and helped to not only feed me, but to also brush my teeth for me. Well, she actually helped me with everything. I was essentially a baby again. She had to bathe me, help me to the restroom, wipe me, feed me (my two orange segments), get everything for me, and DO everything for me. She began forming rock-solid muscles she never knew she had due to lifting me in and out of the bathtub and car, and taking me everywhere I needed to go, like my exciting dates to the sofa or the bed.

FIFTEEN

CHIROPRACTOR

And as it is appointed for men to die once, but after this the judgment.

HEBREWS 9:27
(NKJV)

"Daddy, please help me. Take me somewhere, anywhere, I can get help. Please!" I whisper cried out one day while taking my magical steroid pills that were doing nothing. Since I was now under the care of the on-call doctor and he wouldn't see me again, the only person my dad could think of was our former chiropractor. I say former because he had moved to a different city that was quite the drive to reach, but we still loved him and selfishly wished he had never moved. He was such an amazing chiropractor that he had become a professor at the chiropractic school. He had anointed hands that were bathed in healing and prayer.

"I'm taking you to our old chiropractor, Dr. Turner," my

dad announced and quickly packed me up into his truck. The drive that took just over an hour from our home to the chiropractic school in Pearland was torture, but my steel determination was set—we would make it to our destination no matter what. It had only been a handful of days since starting the steroid pack, and I was so much worse. The light of the sun was excruciating to my sensitive eyes and pounding head. The road movement and noise almost undid me completely but I just hung in there, hoping for answers and relief.

When we arrived, Dr. Turner greeted us at the door and was completely aghast at my state of ill-being and appearance. He knew me as a cheerleader and a runner; strong and full of life. It was his anointed hands that kept my back and joints in line after being tossed in the air day after day on the squad. I could read the question in his eyes: "How can this possibly be the same person?"

I was wheeled back to a dark exam room where my parents and I waited for only a few moments. I was lying down on the chiropractic bed when Dr. Turner entered. He was the opposite of the doctor on call that we had visited. He was loving, warm, compassionate, and gave us his time. He sat with us for as long as we needed.

At this point, it had only been a few weeks since the onset of the migraines that we had originally thought were brought on by the TMJ treatments, and only a handful of days since the "anxiety" and "Bell's palsy" diagnosis, but it felt like an eternity had passed. It felt like an entirely different life. My parents were so wrapped up in the trauma that was their daughter that no one even knew what was going on with me yet. I was all-encompassing. It was the first time someone would hear the short but wild story all the way through.

The doctor sat quietly and listened to all of the details my parents were able to give. They cried, Dr. Turner cried, and I just lay there waiting, hoping for answers.

Dr. Turner left the room momentarily to clear his schedule, then came back to begin a very thorough examination. The first moment he touched me he reached down to my lower leg. He stopped and held it and looked up with tears in his eyes. In awe, he said, "Her muscles are contracting with powerful force." He then proceeded to find that all my muscles were taking turns doing this.

He looked into my eyes and listened to my chest and heart. He performed a slow, gentle, and methodical chiropractic adjustment of my entire body, including my cranium and feet. My bones were so out of joint from the constant pulling and squeezing of my muscles that the adjustment felt amazing. It was a drop of relief in an ocean of pain.

He proceeded to massage my calf and shoulder muscles to help my muscles relax and stop spasming for a short time. Once I was finally aligned, Dr. Turner very systematically proceeded to read my organs and vital signs. I just lay there with my eyes closed, but I know he held different rocks and minerals up to various organ locations on my body and then "read" the results. My body was in the most peaceful state it had been in since this all began.

He wrote all of his notes down, and when he was finished, he began to tell the three of us some shocking facts about my body. He told us in percentages how much of each of my organs was functioning, and the answers he gave were mind-boggling.

My stomach was functioning at a mere 5%—no wonder my body rejected all food and fluids—and my kidneys and liver were functioning somewhere around 15% and 20%. I don't remember the other percentages he shared with us, but he proceeded to tell us about my lungs, gallbladder, intestine, heart, and other vital organs. They were all well below the 50% function mark except for my heart and lungs. God had preserved those two and they were keeping me alive.

Dr. Turner didn't know what was wrong with me. He had no answers, no medications or ideas on what to do, except to get help quickly. My body was shutting down. Time was of the essence.

We left there low. Actually, I left there feeling better, and I continued to feel better for the next few hours now that my muscles were calm and my body was in alignment, but it didn't last long. By evening I was in my former pain and anguish, but those few hours of reprieve were worth the long drive. It was the break I needed to keep fighting.

As we drove home, my parents talked about what the doctor had told them. My mom believed everything Dr. Turner had said about my low-functioning organs. My dad thought the doc was crazy; how could he possibly know what levels my organs were functioning at by looking at some rocks? Later we would find out that the doctor was completely accurate, so whatever he did, gave a true picture of my body's overall health.

I'm not sure what happened once we got home. My parents took me to my bed and I slept a little for the first time in a long time. Slept...really slept. Not passed out. My parents may have slept too, or they may have stayed up talking and praying. I'm not really sure, but what I do know is that everything changed the next day.

After going to the chiropractor and experiencing some short-term relief, things returned to our new and torturous normal. The good thing was that my parents had found time to breathe for a moment and passed on the word that their daughter was very sick. They also asked their best friends, another husband and wife that went to our church, to come over and pray with us the next evening. Maybe the Lord would reveal something to us as we prayed?

The migraine medication didn't work, stopping the TMJ treatment didn't work, and going to the chiropractor helped momentarily but left us with more questions than answers. My official diagnosis was still migraines brought on by the TMJ that caused anxiety attacks and, in turn, Bell's palsy. That prognosis seemed more like a death sentence than what the "diagnosis" suggested.

I was suffocating in this cocoon, and there seemed to be no glimmer of light anymore.

The next evening my parents' best friends came over to pray. When they arrived, they were visibly shocked and shaken by my diminished appearance. They listened to my parents give them the details from the beginning to the present time. Then, they gathered around me as I lay back in my dad's recliner. They prayed. They prayed for wisdom and answers. They prayed for the correct diagnosis and the next steps we should take. They prayed and then, when they were done, they left.

It was getting late and everyone was tired. I stayed in the recliner while my parents bid our friends adieu. Afterward, Mom and Dad went on to do whatever they needed to do in order to get us all ready for bed, and wrap up daily household life and work needs.

That was when I saw him. I was alone in the dim light of our den, lying in the recliner facing the built-in bookshelf where our television, which was off, was housed. From this vantage point I also faced the side door that led out to our driveway. I actually felt him before I saw him. The feeling of him is what made me look up to see who was there.

Standing in the doorway, from the side entry to the den, was the Death Angel. I don't know what else to call him. Maybe the Life Angel instead since he was truly full of love and life instead of fear and death? He was tall and well-built but hidden behind a robe. I couldn't clearly see his facial features, but his eyes were tender and strong. This angel of death (or of life) was not scary or grim, but rather beautiful. His presence flooded me with peace. He stood stone-still and allowed his gaze to lock on to my eyes. That is when he spoke to me. No, he didn't use audible words through his mouth, but I heard him in my mind.

"Are you ready to go home?"

He was here to take me home, but I had a choice. I knew I could go with him to Heaven and end all this misery and pain, or I could stay and fight. What a decision to make at age nineteen. My young life had been so beautiful. Was I ready to go now after having only been ill several weeks? The answer was YES, I was ready to go home. I was in so much pain and so very exhausted.

I had actually begged my mom to kill me one afternoon. While lying on the sofa, I had called my mom over. "Mom. Would you please put me out of my misery? I can't take this pain any longer. It hurts so much, and I am so tired."

"What? No! What are you talking about? You are going to get better."

"Mom, I can't take it. The gun is in the top drawer of the dresser. Bring it here and I'll remind you how to use it. I can go to Heaven. God will forgive you. Please!"

"No. Don't say that!"

"I know where I'm going, and I want to go now. What purpose can I accomplish as a vegetable, in pain, who can't even talk? Just shoot me in the head. I won't even feel it. Please, Mom," I pleaded.

"No. NO!" she shouted before storming out of the room.

Can you imagine your ill child begging you to shoot them in the head? I had reminded her where the gun was. I told her I would remind her how to use it. That is how desperate I was in that moment. Although I would never get a gun and take my own life or the life of another, I sure hoped she would put me out of my misery. I had tried to persuade her that God wouldn't hold it against her for killing me because I would be going to Heaven. He would greet me there and all this pain and torturous suffering would be gone. We had a verbal tug-of-war about why she should kill me versus why she could not and would not. I had begged and begged in my whispered squeak of a voice and she cried and yelled that she wasn't going to listen to me. Then she left the room. She had no choice; I was heaping buckets of agony upon her head with my selfishness.

I was trying to take control of my life instead of letting it play out the way it should. I knew my God, yet I attempted to remove Him from the equation; what a horrible and selfish mistake that would have been. My incessant desire to stop the anguish overrode all of that knowledge in that moment of weakness.

We had no real diagnosis. I had no idea what was wrong with me. There was no hope of getting better from a medical standpoint, and I simply could not imagine living the next year, or twenty years, in the state that I was in currently. My faith was weak but suicide and assisted death is NOT the answer. That would just add insult to injury.

No, the answer is to let go of our flesh and let God do

HIS mighty work of power. We have so based our "medical needs" on the terms of this world that when things get desperate, we have forgotten the loving intentions and power of our Lord. Oh God, forgive us! He has plans for our good and can still use us in any state. His full desire is for our health and healing, He does not make us sick. What a defeated people we have allowed ourselves to become; me included. But one wonderful thing about the Lord is that no matter how much we have forgotten Him in any given moment, He has never forgotten us, and He still chooses to meet us where we are, weak faith and all.

Now the Death Angel was standing before me and giving me a choice. A choice I had longed for and tried to make happen on my own. I could go home. I wanted to go home. I could just simply close my eyes and he would reach out his hand and escort me to the heavenlies. Oh, how I had awaited this moment. Oh, how glorious it would be.

As a Christian who knew where my eternity would be spent, the Death Angel was the most beautiful thing I had seen since the onset of my illness. He was peaceful and filled me with such joy. Yet, in that moment, I simply could not choose. I had a flash of realization that it would crush my parents. I understood that my boyfriend would be scarred and that I would be missing out on some greater plan that my Lord had for me in the life I had yet to live. I was able to think more clearly in this moment than when I had been begging my mom to help me die.

So, instead of choosing for myself, I drank in the peace that this angel had ushered in and called for my mom.

She came running like she always did. Ready to serve and help in any way she could. I don't even remember looking up at her. I'm not sure I did because my eyes were so transfixed on the angel that stood nearby.

"Mom," I said to her in the most calm and clear voice I had used since my paralysis, "I can stay home and die tonight, or we can go to the hospital and fight this thing. You choose."

And choose she did. She jumped high off the ground, screamed louder than I had ever heard her scream before and took off running toward my dad. "Wayman, quick. We need to get Natalie to the hospital. Now!"

The Death Angel took one longer look at me. He very slowly and deliberately gave me one affirmative nod of his head, turned around, and disappeared. He was gone, and now I had to fight for my life.

At the very moment of my mom's decision to "fight this thing," I steeled myself. I would no longer ask for death or pray to be removed from this situation. Yes, I would pray for healing, but I would move forth in grace and love, and I would fight until my healing was manifested. I would not complain about the pain or process, I would simply endure and obey.

True bravery is not the absence of fear, but the realization that fear has no hold on you with God. I would be brave, remembering the love of the Lord. Inside my small, dark chrysalis, the real change was about to begin: the transformative wonder that creates wings. All those faith-building years were going to be put to use and one day I was going to fly.

SIXTEEN

HOSPITAL

*But you, Lord, are a shield around me, my glory, the
One who lifts my head high. I call out to the Lord,
and he answers me from his holy mountain.
Arise, Lord! Deliver me, my God! Strike all my
enemies on the jaw; break the teeth of the wicked.
From the Lord comes deliverance. May your blessing
be on your people.*

PSALM 3:3-4, 7-8
(NIV)

A s we rushed to the hospital in the middle of the night,
it was eerily quiet on the roads. The blacktop pavement drove smooth under our tires, and the red lights shone
brightly on our windshield. I suppose not much is going on
in small town America in the middle of the night.

"Run the red lights, Dad. There are no cars. I'm dying."

"I could get pulled over and that would slow us down
even more." His voice trembled.

"So slow down at the intersection and honk your horn. No one is out here. I am going to die before we get there."

I felt everything inside me shutting down and knew there was not much time.

After what seemed like an eternity, we pulled in front of the ER doors and I was wheeled inside. A bustle of activity exploded around me. I presume it is never quiet in the ER, even if the night outside seems calm. My body had begun to crash, so it was very difficult for me to respond to any of the questions the nurses began throwing at me. I don't actually remember responding to the questions at all.

My eyes began to gloss over and I started to sink into my wheelchair. I could hear my mom talking frantically while trying to fill out paperwork when I suddenly began to tremble with a small seizure. I was quickly transferred onto a gurney. Almost the moment my body hit the bed, I began to convulse violently. I was whisked away to a room where it took several men to hold me down as I flopped like a fish, throwing my arms and legs off the bed.

"She's crashing," a female voice yelled out.

"Grab hold of her," a man called.

"I can't place this IV with her convulsing. Hold her tighter," another woman's voice commanded.

"Honey, what drug did you take? Can you tell me what you are overdosing on?" a nurse questioned me over and over again as she slapped my face.

"I'm not on any drugs. I didn't overdose," I was trying to tell her even as my eyes were rolling back in my head, but the words would not move from my mind to my lips.

"She's not on any drugs. She isn't overdosing!" my mom yelled. "Please listen to me, she's not on any drugs!" She begged them to listen to her about my medical history, but it seemed the room was suddenly out of control, filled with nurses, doctors, and panic.

At some point an IV finally found its way into my arm, and they pumped copious amounts of fluids into me along with morphine, Benadryl, and some other long-forgotten medications. After a while my body calmed, and the men were able to let go of me and leave the room. My eyes cleared and I was able to speak again in my whispered squeak croak of a voice. This was a night of torment. If I hadn't had the visit from the Death/Life Angel I would have given up that night, but due to the "deal" we made, I was prepared to fight...even if that meant lying on a gurney, being treated as if I was overdosing on drugs and hooked up to various tubes.

After my body calmed down, I lay quietly in my room just waiting. For what? I'm not sure.

"Do you want me to call Wayne?" my dad asked me, his voice full of weary defeat.

"Yes. Call him and let him know. He needs to know," I said, having suddenly remembered that I had a boyfriend.

Wayne came to the ER that night and finally found out all the craziness that had been going on. I had not just been sick; I had been dying. From this moment on, Wayne stuck to me like glue whenever he could. After work, he would come over and just sit with me while I lay on the sofa or in a hospital bed. When he went back to the University of Texas, he would drive home on the weekends to sit in my hospital room with me and hold my hand. Along with my parents' unyielding support, his presence helped prod me along.

As it so happened, the hospital listed my doctor as the on-call doctor that had misdiagnosed me thus far, and his care over me in this short hospital stay was equally as bad. I asked to see a neurologist and was again denied and released, only to end up repeating the same horrors several days later and ending up back in the hospital ER in the middle of the night.

The second time they admitted me into the hospital and gave me a shared room NOT in the intensive care unit (ICU). I was in a regular room even though I was unable to sit up on my own, feed myself, walk or do pretty much anything. I have no idea what the on-call doctor had put in my charts, but it kept me from having tests run and from seeing a neurologist. I was sent home yet again after just a few nights.

I was so scared to stay in the hospital alone without one of my parents. I was prone to vomiting up fluids, but as I was unable to sit up when that happened, I needed someone to pull me to a sitting position to keep me from choking. The hospital would not let my parents stay. I was not even strong enough to press the nurses' call button or the buttons on my bed that would raise me up. They barely checked on me.

I had only two nurses check on me in the three days I stayed there. They simply ignored me, like I was a strung-out addict detoxing from drugs long enough to be sent home and return again on a repeat cycle. No compassion whatso-ever, even if I had been coming off a high.

One night, I remember my dad leaving me his Nextel phone with the walkie-talkie capability. I tried for hours to push that button to talk to them, but my lack of strength and coordination would not allow my fingers to cooperate.

I was fragile, alone, scared and in a very dark place. Literally—the room I was in was dark. The lights were never turned on and the curtains over the window were never drawn open. With no nurses checking on me by night, and my so-called doctor never checking on me during the day, I felt helpless. All I could do was cry out to God for help and answers.

God heard my cry as I lay alone, wrapped in my silk cocoon. He heard my cry and answered me, but not until a precious gift was given to me.

SEVENTEEN

BIRTHDAY

To appoint unto them that mourn in Zion, to give unto them beauty for ashes, the oil of joy for mourning, the garment of praise for the spirit of heaviness; that they might be called trees of righteousness, the planting of the Lord, that he might be glorified.

ISAIAH 61:3
KJV

Between hospital visits I had my birthday. I had such different plans for myself at age twenty. I saw myself finishing up my senior year of college and going off to a premed program of some kind, or maybe starting a rewarding career in the sciences. I certainly did not see myself fighting for my life. Definitely not paralyzed and completely dependent on others. Certainly not trapped and lonely and leaning solely on God for everything. God alone! For He was the only one that could sustain me.

There was one other thing that helped—my parents began taking me to get massages from a church friend of ours, Joanna Aluotto. Joanna was a massage therapist with anointed hands. I went to her as often as possible to help me get an hour or more of relief. I would lie on her massage table in a warm room filled with soft worship music. She would then gently yet firmly work all the knots and pain out of my muscles that the charley horses had put there. Often times, I could hear her praying for me under her breath as she worked her gifted hands along my aching muscles. It was so comforting that I would nearly fall asleep during each session, and that reprieve would help keep me going until I could see her again.

After one such massage the realization came to me that I had forgotten my own birthday. I didn't know what month we were in, much less the date, but my mom remembered. Somehow, between all the craziness of the last few weeks, she had been setting up a surprise for me.

I'm sure her motives were manifold. One, it may be my last birthday ever. Two, I needed to see people and their love for me. I needed encouragement. Three, I needed to briefly let go of the urgent, painful moments that stayed at the forefront of my mind, and to just stop to have "fun."

Mommy threw me a surprise party. I don't know how she was able to pull it off. Apparently, after she tucked me away in bed each night, she would stay up late to make phone calls to family and friends. She had everyone spread the word that I was very sick and that she was throwing a surprise birthday party for me. "Come if you can" spread by word of mouth. She cooked up party foods, had a cake made, and cleaned and decorated the house. All behind my back.

I believe it was during this "party planning" time that my brother, Wayman Jr., learned about my illness. He dropped whatever it was he was doing and drove down from Fort Worth to see me.

My brother and I had always loved each other but had also always been distant. Brother, as I called him, is actually my half brother from a different mom. He is thirteen years older than I am, and we were raised in different homes.

We had finally been getting closer just before my illness. Our age difference didn't seem like such a chasm anymore, and when I was at Baylor, in Waco, I lived much closer to him and his wife. I was able to come babysit his precious new son on occasion while up at college.

Brother didn't know this, but as a young kiddo I had a crush on him. When I was around four years old, I would tell my parents that I was going to marry him when I grew up. They assured me that my feelings would change, but I insisted that I l-o-v-e-d him.

I remember standing on my driveway, waiting for him to come visit. When I would see his car coming, I would get so excited. He would finally stop the engine, climb out of his car, and walk towards me while I would run up to him, fling my arms around his neck, and hug him with my tiny, chubby hands. I was always thrilled to see him, and I thought he was the most handsome man I had ever seen. Well, when you are four and your half brother is seventeen, he is a man in your eyes. Oh, the sweet innocence of a child.

My brother heard that I might die and came down to see me. I was excited and relieved to see him but was unable to express it as I had when I was a child. I remember him plopping down on the sofa next to me with his big smile and saying, "Hey, Sissy, stop going around scaring everyone." I watched his eyes turn red and fill up with tears before he turned away, got up, and walked out of the room. Yes, I love my brother, and it was hard to see all that emotion on his face. But I needed to see him, and he loved me well over the next few days.

I woke up on the morning of my birthday, not knowing it would be different than any other day. I still couldn't eat and remained in tremendous incessant pain. I was still paralyzed and wasn't strong enough to lift my head up to make eye contact.

Around lunchtime, I was lying on the sofa in our den trying to concentrate on anything other than the pain I was in. I heard the doorbell ring and the soft talking of people. I listened as the front door of our home began to open and close repeatedly, even though I could not see that door from the sofa in the den. Our formal living room and dining room were an open-concept floor plan that the front door led directly into via an open foyer. Then around a wall was the kitchen and breakfast room, which the den sat off. Our entry, dining, and living room area was quite large and could hold a great crowd of people. And a rather sizable crowd had begun to form.

My mom popped into the den where I was lying. She had a big smile on her face and Wayne by her side. Wayne was holding balloons, red roses, and a birthday present for me. I was so surprised to see him, with his signature Cheshire cat grin and gifts, for I had not remembered it was my birthday. After taking a picture of Wayne and me together, my mom stated, "I have a surprise for you in the other room."

Mommy corralled my arms into cooperating and put my fluffy pink bathrobe on me since I was always cold and snuggled under several layers of blankets. Then she settled me into my wheelchair and rolled me into the formal living room/dining room.

"Surprise! Happy Birthday!" came a chorus of voices.

After my initial surprise, Mom parked me near the front door by the dining table, which was filled with food and decorations, before trotting off to play hostess. I was overwhelmed. Yes, I still hurt and felt like death, but so many people came and went over the next several hours. They brought flowers, smiles, prayers, and love.

I was floored by who all came. People I would have never thought had any concern toward me showed up. We recognized each other from church or days past, but they came. They came and came and came. Those I knew well and those I barely knew at all. Everyone wanted to know what was wrong. What happened? Would I get better? All questions we didn't have the answer to.

As I sat looking at the ground in my wheelchair, I had many people come over to talk to me. They would talk TO me—not at me, not around me, but to me. I couldn't answer their questions, talk back, or make eye contact, but they continued to talk to me even though it was often my mom, dad, brother, or Wayne answering them and conversing on my behalf. That was huge. So very important. I learned something in that moment: just because a person is disabled and unable to respond, it doesn't mean they can't hear and understand, or even answer your questions in their own mind. Being treated like a properly functioning and smart individual is so incredibly essential.

After the birthday festivities were over, I was completely exhausted from doing nothing but sitting. I was ushered back into the den and made comfortable under my pile of blankets on the sofa. While Wayne and I watched my new birthday movie, my brother came over and said,

"Hey, Sissy, I need to run out really quickly for something. You gonna be okay while I'm gone?"

He returned with a bouquet of sunflowers and told me, "I got you sunflowers. They are my favorite flower because they are so happy and remind me of the sun." Of all the beautiful flowers I received that day, and in the weeks to come, those sunflowers were my favorite.

EIGHTEEN

MY REAL DOCTOR

*The name of the Lord is a strong tower; the righteous
run to it and are safe.*

PROVERBS 18:10

(NKJV)

The birthday festivities were a wonderful reprieve from what had become an agonizing existence. Wonderful didn't last long. The madness of emergency hospital visits and my body crashing off and on began again, and after being released from the hospital a third time without any answers, we decided that this had gone on long enough. No more! No more visits to the on-call doctor. No more midnight visits to the ER. No more madness. We needed answers now.

After making our way home from yet another ER visit, drained and deflated, my mom paced the house waiting for daylight so she could call my doctor at her personal residence. My REAL doctor.

Around 5:30 a.m., my mother could wait no longer and made the pleading phone call. She had the ear of MY doctor, who had me come into her office immediately, before business hours began. After all, she had just seen me a handful of weeks ago for a migraine headache...what could have possibly happened since? A lot. A whole lot had happened.

Next thing I knew, I was loaded up in the car and off we went. Mom wheeled me up to the office, into the lobby and then...gasp! Shock! Silence!

"What on earth has happened? Who is this young lady in the wheelchair? This is not our patient, not the person from several weeks ago. This is not possible!" the doctors cried aloud.

The look of shock on my doctor and physician assistant's faces was enough to know that something was really wrong. They looked horrified, allowing their emotions to flash across their faces. Years of medical training in bedside manners couldn't disguise their astonished appearances.

Last they knew, I was sent home with a migraine diagnosis. I was wheeled back to the hallway to begin the standard check-in procedures. I had lost fourteen pounds in just a few weeks due to starvation. I was now a mere eighty-nine pounds, which is nothing for my 5'3" stature. That alone should have sent up red flags to the hospital I had so frequently visited, but in their eyes I was a delusional drug addict, suffering from Bell's palsy brought on by panic attacks. I was not someone to be taken seriously, although everyone should be taken seriously, drug addict or not. God loves everyone and wants to pour out His love and healing power on each and every person.

Not only was the weight loss a red flag, but I was also

paralyzed. My face didn't work; half of it drooped. I couldn't stand on my own and needed help getting onto the scale. I couldn't walk. I looked emaciated and hollow. My skin was pale and ashen, and I had broken out in acne that had never been an issue in the past. My eyes floated in different directions and were unable to focus without me seeing double or triple vision. It was all nauseating and simply not me.

Something was definitely wrong, and it took one look from my real doctor to know that we were dealing with something bigger than migraines, TMJ, Bell's palsy or anxiety attacks. Disease was devouring me from the inside out. But what could that disease be?

I was wheeled back to a room and my mom dictated our entire story again. This time to my doctor, Dr. Martinez, and her physician's assistant, Amy. They listened carefully while a full range of emotions played out on their faces. They were outraged that the on-call doctor had not notified them. They were part of a team of doctors in a medical group and were supposed to be notified if a patient of theirs was seen when they were not on call. They were incensed that Dr. On Call had taken over my care entirely, telling us not to come back to our normal doctor. They were appalled that no formal tests had been performed. And they were scared that they might be too late to intervene.

Dr. Martinez took my parents to a different room, to talk to them in private about my condition and what steps we would take going forward. Amy stayed with me.

Amy had been my PA for quite some time, so we had a good rapport. As I gazed at the floor watching it move and morph before me, becoming two and three floors and then back to one solid floor again, I croaked at her to give it to me straight. "What could we possibly be looking at?" I asked.

And she was honest with me. It was so refreshing. I was instantly filled with hope. Not because anything she suggested was good—actually, they were all pretty much death sentences—but because they were possible answers, and someone was finally going to take me seriously.

Hope is an incredible thing. It can uphold a person in the very worst of times. Illnesses like cancer, multiple sclerosis, Lou Gehrig's disease (ALS), Huntington's and other horrible diseases were given as a list of possibilities of what could be attacking me, but even in hearing that list I was filled with hope. The hope of being cared for. The hope of being listened to, heard, and understood. The hope that whatever future I had left, no matter how long or short, that someone would be fighting for me and not against me. And yes, even the hope of a possible healing or cure.

My parents came back into my room, their faces having been washed with tears, looking a bit hopeless instead of hopeful. Thinking back, maybe they were just weary from the battle and ready to pass the baton to someone that might actually have answers. They hugged me and stood around waiting for our next move. No words were spoken, only anticipation and longing filled the silent weightiness of the room. My doctor's office was in a hospital building (not the same hospital I had been rushed to repeatedly already), so she had me immediately admitted and called for a...wait for it...you guessed it...a neurologist!

My parents went to admissions to fill out paperwork while I was sent up to a room. After only a few minutes of sitting alone, my pastor, Gary, and his wife, Lori, walked into my room. How did they find out I was in the hospital so quickly? Turns out that they were already in the hospital when they saw my parents down in admissions. That was a God thing! They came up to check on me. We even cracked a few jokes while I stared down at their shoes and the speckled laminate tile floors, waiting to be wheeled off to get an MRI of the brain. They were just who I needed to see. The concern in their eyes and the love in their voices was just what my dry and thirsty soul needed before the upcoming barrage of medical tests.

Before my parents had finished in admissions, a nurse arrived to wheel me down to imaging. I figured they would either come find me or just wait in my room but didn't give them much thought. What I do remember is sitting silently as the wheelchair wheels squeaked and grabbed at the floor. I was contemplating all that had transpired up until that moment. There was much to remember, think about, and give over to God; much to worship and praise Him for as I set out on this new leg of my journey. I was hopeful that it was almost time to break out of my cocoon but didn't realize that I had several more weeks of transformation ahead of me.

I rode along the never-ending sterile hallways and down the large humming elevator to imaging. Not a word was spoken by either the nurse or myself. I simply sat in silence and rested in the competent hands of those helping me.

Once in imaging, a technician set me on the patient table of the MRI bed and prepped me for the test. I had never had an MRI before, so as I slumped forward, he patiently explained to me what I would be experiencing.

After giving me all of the instructions and disclosures, I had to sign a waiver. How does a paralyzed person with no fine motor skills sign a waiver? Hanging my head low I whispered, "I can't. I can't write."

It was a moment of defeat for me. I had been fighting and struggling to hold it all together, and I had promised to endure with grace, but how could I be graceful when I could not do what was asked and required of me?

The power of the Lord flooded that small MRI room. His love—God's love—began to flow over me, as this technician became Jesus in human flesh and blood. He personally became the hands and feet of Christ on my behalf. He served me selflessly in my time of need and humility. With compassion in his eyes, he gently placed the pen in my hand and held the clipboard up to the tip of the pen so I could attempt to squiggle my name. I eked out something resembling chicken scratch that looked nothing like my signature. I had not realized until that moment that I had even lost my signature, that which had become my handwriting and part of my identity. Something so basic yet so defining was gone. Everything that I had become in the physical body, down to the smallest details of my voice and signature, had been taken from me. I was a broken individual, and I would never be the same again.

I had to remind myself that the things I thought made up who I was—my voice, my signature, my accomplishments, my body, and so many other details that when put together created Natalie, were actually NOT my identity. They were my characteristics. My identity was in Christ. As long as I have Him, I am who I am supposed to be. Walking (or lying there unable to move) down the path of my life and bringing Him glory each moment of the day, makes me who I am. Not my will, but His will be done.

Before laying me back and moving me into the MRI tube, the technician asked if I had any metal in or on my body. "If you have any metal, it will be violently ripped out of you. We don't want that to happen," he whispered. Like a flash of memory through my mind, I remembered that the hair band I had been wearing to hold my hair up in the same messy bun for an unnumbered amount of days contained a metal tag.

"Um yeah. My hair band...my ponytail holder has metal on it," I croaked and squeaked out the best I could while staring down at my knees.

"Do you think you can remove it?" the technician asked sympathetically.

"No, my arms won't cooperate. I'm trying to raise them but they aren't moving," I dejectedly replied.

So this male technician, who was so full of tenderness, gently reached up and removed my hair band for me. My long, and probably very greasy, hair came tumbling down around my shoulders in a mass of tangles and curls. But the technician was not finished there. He continued to smooth my hair back and down into a semblance of respectability so I wouldn't feel so unkempt.

"What about your earplugs? Do you think you can put those in, or would you like me to help you with those?" he questioned sympathetically, even though he already knew the answer.

Feeling overcome, I shook my head to indicate that I was indeed not able to place my earplugs in myself. I was still staring down at my knees with my back hunched over; I didn't have the strength to even attempt to look up at him. I don't know how he perceived the slight negative shake of my head, with me all hunched over and my hair hanging around me, but he understood. He squatted down to look me in the eyes with such compassion I felt I would melt. Very tenderly and thoughtfully, he brushed my hair aside and put the earplugs in my ears, taking extra time and care to be sure they were securely in place, and redoing them several times just to be sure. He fussed over me like I was his own daughter as a single tear escaped my right eye and trickled down my cheek.

Ever so gently, he laid me back on the patient table, fixed my long hair around me, walked out of the room, and closed the door. In those moments I had felt how I could only assume the disciples felt when Jesus washed their feet: fully vulnerable yet fully loved and cared for. It's hard to fathom how a moment before a medical procedure could be intimate, but I can only explain that moment as such. Not with the technician and myself, but between my God and His daughter—me.

As I lay on that table, I closed my eyes, prayed, and sang worship songs in my mind. I felt the table slide my body back into the tube.

"The test is about to begin. Just lie still so we get a good reading," came the technician's voice over the loud speaker. Next came a series of loud clicks and whirrs as the machine worked and I rested in the Lord. I fully relaxed my body into the arms of Christ.

It's amazing what comes flooding back to your memory in a time of scheduled seclusion. So many memorized scripture verses from the Bible, so many other verses read only a handful of times and previously forgotten, all those worship songs sung repeatedly in chapel during my private school days, and all of those many, many miracles God had performed in my previous caterpillar life. Each one came flooding back to me as I lay resting and waiting.

I replayed friendships, laughter, and joyful memories, and I worshipped the Lord in my cocoon. As I lay in that tube for over an hour, hearing the loud clicks, beeps, and whirrs of the machine reading my brain and searching for answers, I was comforted by my younger caterpillar days.

The days where I had eaten the fruits of God's gifts, the days where I had grown and become fat. The days before I knew anything would ever go wrong with my body. Maybe those were my romance days walking with the Lord? The days He wooed me into His arms of love knowing full well that I would need His full strength to carry me through this trial.

NINETEEN

AN ORANGE

Be strong and courageous. Do not be afraid or terri-
fied because of them, for the Lord your God goes with
you; He will never leave you nor forsake you.

DEUTERONOMY 31:6

(NIV)

Once the MRI was complete, I saw that my parents had found me in imaging.

"Well, it looks like you still have a brain in there," the technician and my dad both quipped. I attempted to laugh, but it came out more as a gurgle. Oh well, at least I still had some humor left.

I was wheeled back to my temporary hospital room, and Dr. Martinez and Amy came to see me. They let me know that not only would they be checking on me frequently, but that they were handing my care over to the neurologist on their team, Dr. Diaz.

"You should be expecting a visit from Dr. Diaz any

minute. You will like him. He is very kind and gentle, and he knows his stuff," reassured Dr. Martinez.

The doctors had apparently already debriefed Dr. Diaz about my symptoms and were fairly certain that they knew what was going on, but a few more tests and a once-over by Dr. Diaz needed to take place first. I was not privy to any of their speculations yet, so was still uncertain as to my condition's mortality rate.

They were right—what seemed like only a short time later my new neurologist came bouncing into my room. He was filled with joy and laughter and had a huge smile on his face. I was curious as to what he could possibly be so happy about considering the hell I had been going through. He decided to let me in on a little secret. The first words out of his mouth were, "Great news! You are not going to die! I know what is wrong with you."

Whoosh! It felt like all of the air had been knocked out of my lungs upon hearing those fateful words. The truth was, I should have already been dead several times over, and the road to recovery would be very hard and could leave me with lifelong "issues," but they told me that much later. At that point, the neurologist was all sunshine and rainbows, underplaying the severity to help aid the beginning of my recovery process.

Dr. Diaz pulled a chair in front of my stooped body. I was sitting at the edge of a hospital bed with my legs dangling over the side, and he pulled out his cute little rubber hammer to check my reflexes. He struck my knee looking for that "knee jerk" reaction. I had none. I actually giggled when my leg refused to respond to his mallet. It felt strange for my leg to continue to dangle when it should have swung back and forth. He also checked my wrists, elbows, and ankles...nothing.

He looked into my floating eyes, examined my drooping face, which now held no creases or wrinkles because my muscles were completely lax, and then he handed me an orange. "Keep this orange safe for me because I am going to need it," he stated matter-of-factly, just before leaving my room. He probably set off to find my parents who had not returned to my room with me after the MRI as they were completing more paperwork.

I was left alone in that hospital room with my legs flopping over the side of the bed, my head and shoulders wilting down, and holding and orange in my non-responsive hand. Good thing Dr. Diaz curled my fingers around that orange. I was having difficulty holding on to that curiously required object. I was nervous about dropping said orange just in case he really did need it, but I couldn't get up to set it anywhere safe. So there I sat, hunched over with this mysterious orange for some unknown reason. Looking back, I now find it ironic that the fruit he handed me was an orange considering that was the only food I had successfully held down. But in that moment, I just kept telling myself to not drop the orange.

When Dr. Diaz returned, he sat down on the bed next to me and began to tell me why his orange was so important. About halfway into his monologue of explaining the relationship between a spinal tap and an orange, my mom walked into the room looking like she had been hit with a wrecking ball. I am sure the full gamut of emotions she endured that day made her feel like she had been wrung out wet and left to dry. But she also looked nervous and uncertain about this joyful neurologist sitting beside me. The doctor had yet to tell her about his thoughts on what was ailing me. She had not yet heard the "You're not going to die" words, so when she entered the room, she verbally replayed our story to Dr. Diaz as he sat and listened patiently. It was like she regurgitated the narrative by rote after having told it so many times recently. Dr. Diaz smiled and gave her the good news that he thought I was going to live and, over time, hopefully even recover.

Then he dropped the bomb.

He told us about the tests he would have to run to confirm his diagnosis. After everything else my mom had endured of late, she didn't particularly want to have to endure these next steps too. She sat down on the other side of me while the doctor took his orange away because he now needed it. Then he pulled out a syringe and showed me how he practices performing spinal taps with that orange. Oh! That's what was coming next—I had to have a spinal tap, and my mom had to help hold me in the correct position. I wasn't strong enough to hold myself in any particular position, so I just slumped or flopped wherever my body settled. My mom's complexion turned a little ashen, but she steeled herself for the task at hand.

I was moved further to the edge of the bed and placed in a sort of cannonball position, with my mom in front of me holding my legs up to my chest with her body, and my head and back down over my knees. I'm kind of surprised she didn't faint having to watch the doctor perform this procedure on her daughter, but she can be as tough as nails when the moment calls for it. I felt the doctor put his orange on my back, I heard him tell me I would feel a prick and voila... that was that. He was so practiced and quick that all I really felt were my mom's icy hands wrapped around my back and that cold orange against my skin. When Dr. Diaz was done, he peeled the orange, ate it, and told me I had to lie down flat on my back for at least the next hour.

During that hour of lying still and waiting, so much

happened. Not necessarily in the physical, but in the spiritual. First, I needed to go to the bathroom but wasn't allowed to get up; too bad I didn't go before the spinal tap. I had IV fluids being pumped into me and I really needed to pee. I couldn't seem to relax enough to use the bedpan; seriously, who can relax enough to use a bedpan? So they had to administer a catheter. Not fun! I do not recommend ever needing a catheter but, wow, what a relief.

My diagnosis came in as I lay as still as a corpse. The lack of reflexes, drooping face, no wrinkles, paralysis, pain, wandering and floating eyes, tingling hands and feet, arthritis and all the rest of the symptoms coupled with the spinal tap confirmation...I had Guillain-Barré syndrome. Finally! A name to put with the illness, and it wasn't a disease, it was a syndrome.

I didn't know what that actually meant and wouldn't find out until the next day but, hey, I had a diagnosis. A correct diagnosis. Praise the Lord!!!

Not only did my diagnosis come in, but since I was in a new hospital and they had never seen a Guillain-Barré patient before, they were not equipped to take care of my needs. Oh no! That was not good. This new hospital, Christus St. Catherine's, was only minutes from my house, so my parents could easily come and go. It was clean and peaceful, and all the nurses and technicians had been wonderful in the face of my storm.

The doctors and the hospital wanted to transfer me to Memorial City Hospital, which was located in a congested part of town, much further from my home, and didn't have the best reputation (although now it seems much improved). At the time, we had several friends sporting personal horror stories from staying there. We prayed. While an ambulance was being prepared to transport me to Memorial City, we prayed that God would work a miracle to keep me where I was. Prayed He would prepare the way for me to receive the care I needed, all while staying close to home in this clean and somewhat cheery environment.

I was lying flat on my back on a gurney. An ambulance was being prepared for my transfer. We were praying. The hour of lying flat on my back came and went, but I simply remained in my prone position. The sun set— brilliant pinks, oranges, and golds outside my window. The room darkened. And time kept ticking by.

Nothing was happening.

I could see red and blue flashing lights, bouncing off the ceiling in my room from the ambulance waiting outside for me. It was getting later and later until we were well into the evening hours.

My mom asked a nurse what was going on and we were informed that while the ambulance was being prepared for my transfer, the hospital had held an emergency board meeting about my case. They determined that although I was the first Guillain-Barré patient they had ever received, I would not be the last, so they decided to go ahead and purchase the equipment necessary for my treatments, and also to try and find a specialist they could contract to run those machines. It was all approved. They were just waiting to hear back from the specialist about his schedule.

Wow! We prayed and God quickly and miraculously answered. I would stay at Christus, keep my neurologist, remain close to home, and have the treatments I needed.

That night I was moved into a private room in the ICU and my mom was allowed to stay with me. They didn't make her leave like the other hospital had. She could stay and I could feel safe.

TWENTY

GUILLAIN-BARRÉ SYNDROME

*Create in me a pure heart, O God, and renew a stead-
fast spirit within me.*

PSALM 51:10
(NIV)

D r. Diaz stopped by the next morning to tell us all about Guillain-Barré syndrome (GBS), pronounced *gee-yan-buh-rey* after the last names of the two men that discovered it. Basically, it can begin after any illness, surgery, vaccination, or anything else that causes your body to begin a "fight" reaction.

He concluded with what he believed was 100% certainty that the third shot in my hepatitis B vaccination series was what kicked off the Guillain-Barré in my body. Immunizations are the number one cause of Guillain-Barré syndrome. Typically, you will see the first symptoms thirty days after the incident, illness, or injury and it will progress from there. My case was unique in that it did begin thirty days after that last vaccination, but instead of hitting me hard immediately, my body continued on a yo-yo pattern before completely succumbing to the attack. I had actually been fighting it during my last semester at Baylor University before coming home for the summer, not simply fighting the flu like I thought.

The body begins the "fight" process of killing off an illness, virus, or bacteria of some kind, and once that invader has been successfully defeated, the white blood cells of the immune system go into overdrive and begin to attack its own body's peripheral nervous system. The nervous system controls everything in the body, thus the strange weakness, paralysis, tingling, pain, and other symptoms.

Guillain-Barré can be mild and short lived, or it can be severe, even causing death. In other countries, death occurs more often than recovery due to the lack of medical help available. Many people recover fully while others go on with their lives in a wheelchair, needing lifelong assistance. Death often occurs with the heart or lungs paralyzing.

If you are one of the ones who recover, the fullness of healing is typically complete within seven years or less of the onset of symptoms. Fortunately for me, Dr. Diaz had seen many cases of GBS and was very familiar with the syndrome. Unfortunately, mine was the worst case he had seen to date, most likely due to me being misdiagnosed for so long.

As he provided my care over the next weeks, he often shared with me stories of his other patients (excluding their names, of course), and would remark that he was in awe of how gracefully I was enduring such an egregious event. My grace was by the refinement of God alone.

Dr. Diaz had watched grown men reduced to weeping

and despair with lighter cases of GBS than I was afflicted with. As I listened to his recounting of patients' stories, my heart began to burn with compassion for each of them and for anyone else going through this dreadful condition. I knew that if I made it through this alive, I wanted to encourage and help others, but for now I could pray while lying on my back, simply trying to survive myself.

It was a new dawn. Surely it was time to break out of this dark, tight cocoon. Surely I was rounding the corner to better days now that I had my diagnosis and my treatment was to begin. Surely.

Not quite. Since my body had been shutting down for quite some time without the proper medical care, I began spiraling downward even more quickly. My organs were struggling to keep my body working and needed all the help they could get. I was immediately put on a huge bag of vitamin fluids that were neon yellow. I affectionately called it my banana bag because of its color.

I was also put on a regular dose of morphine, both the oral form and a topical patch. Unfortunately, my nerves had been so damaged that the high doses of morphine simply did not touch the pain, but I continued to take it in hopes that it would eventually kick in and do its job.

Having not eaten in weeks, I was also given a few IV bags of potassium. Whoa! Steer clear of IV potassium at all costs. That stuff burns like fire flooding the veins in an attempt to burn out all impurities. No matter how fast or slow the nurses made the drip, the inferno continued. I thought my arm was going to burst into flames, but thankfully I still have my arm without burns to prove that you can survive a bag (or three) of potassium.

I was also prescribed Ensure to drink. What a laugh. I had tried every single combination of food possible over the weeks and was only able to keep down two orange wedges every few hours. Now they wanted me to drink three to five cans of Ensure each day, along with eight glasses of water.

You should have seen the dietician. She was so sweet and well meaning. She was in perfect shape and had the perfectly presentable yet comfortable business clothes. With a brilliant smile on her face, she cracked that first can of chocolate Ensure, stuck a bendy straw in it, held it up to my lips and asked me to drink it, obviously thinking she had solved all of my weight loss and malnutrition woes. With each sip I took, she encouraged me to drink more, and more. Between sips, I attempted to warn her about the volcanic violence that would inevitably happen next. She just nodded and encouraged me even more until I had about a quarter of the can of liquid problem solver ingested. You should have seen the look on her face when that quarter of a can came woefully back up. With no bowl in my lap to catch the mess, I had to have a complete wardrobe and bedsheet change, along with a sponge bath. Now I not only hated peanut butter, but thanks to the overly cheerful and confident dietician, my relationship with chocolate was also beginning to wane.

My trusty dietician and faithful nurses would not give up. They kept trying to coax the stuff down me over the next few days. After that first attempt, I never got more than two sips past my lips before my body began its liquid-rejecting ritual. Thus, my nourishment going forward consisted of sucking on ice chips, my banana bag, the occasional slice of orange, and an occasional bag of liquid inferno potassium. Hey, this was more than I had ingested in weeks, so I should have been feeling great, yet the weight loss persisted and I was getting weaker by the day.

Every time the nurses weighed me, I weighed in lower

than the time before. I was wasting away before their eyes and they would beg me to eat. I was starving. Literally. I wanted to eat more than they wanted me to eat, but they were the ones begging for me to comply while crying real tears, on their knees, beside my bed. They acted like I was their own child or sister. The care of nurses is tremendous. They put their hearts on the line for their patients and have a brickload of emotional investment. They were created to be healers, not to watch someone wither and die. I'm sure that with each passing of a patient, a piece of a nurse's heart goes with them.

I had begun refusing to even try to eat or drink. It took too much energy for me to put forth the wearying effort of nourishment for my body, to waste even more energy having my stomach reject it. It was just easier to not try at all and continue with a hollow pit in my gut.

Starvation is horrible. I weep when I think about starving people around the world. I never understood the magnitude of starvation before Guillain-Barré, but now I have experienced it. It is a slow, painful, and desperate death. The stomach always feels empty, yet heavy with the weight of need. Your joints ache and muscles painfully atrophy without the nourishment they so desperately need. The constant hunger is maddening and thinking about food is torturous. So just ignoring it was what I did. Actually, starvation marked me for the long haul. Even now, as I write my story, I don't like the feeling of being hungry. I love to share my food if it is my idea, but when someone comes and takes food off my plate without asking, it triggers something inside of me. So, yeah, I am a bit possessive over food after having survived literal starvation. But at the same time, it leaves me yearning to feed those without food; the very basic of needs.

One day my favorite nurse, Glen, knelt beside my bed and said that he had asked the doctor to order me a feeding tube. "Okay. I can try that," I thought, but I was going to make a deal first. Since I had been admitted into the ICU, I had a captive audience in the nurses and Glen, this amazing male nurse kneeling beside my bed, would become one of my two favorite nurses during my stay.

Since my Death Angel experience, the cry of my heart had changed. It was no longer about me, but about Him. Change me, mold me, shape me, and make me more like You, Lord. I would spend my days telling of God's glory. Psalm 146:2 (NLT) had become my anthem: "I will praise the Lord as long as I live. I will sing praises to my God with my dying breath."

Nurse Glen told me all about his life and his dreams, and I continually witnessed to him about the Lord and God's plans for him. Maybe one reason he became a favorite nurse was because, in addition to being gentle and kind, he learned to understand my strange toddler voice and we could talk whenever I was able to muster up enough vigor.

As I had been witnessing to him, I learned that he was indeed a Christian, but had been slipping into the "casual" Christian way of living and not loving Jesus like he should. His latest adventure down backslide road was moving in with his girlfriend. As we built a rapport, he began to confide in me that he wanted to be zealous for the Lord like I was. He admitted that he had asked to be put on my rotation because he was drawn to the fire of God that shone out of me, and was attracted to the grace with which I had been going through this deathbed hell.

According to Glen, the entire hospital staff and crew were talking about me. Hmm...I thought he was just trying to give me a reason to live, but no, he was telling the truth. Apparently, God was shining through me and peace had permeated my hospital room. People were talking about the paralyzed girl in ICU and the God she served. He admired my persistent yet loving witness toward him and he wanted to change. He was ready to catch the vision God had for him, but he was scared to do it.

"Let's make a deal. I am now a mere eighty-three pounds and need a food intervention. You want to live the life God has for you and need a spiritual intervention. I will accept the feeding tube being administered if you will go home tonight and explain to your girlfriend your new conviction and arrange to move out, while inviting her to come alongside you in your intentional walk with the Lord," I bargained.

"What if she thinks I'm crazy? What if she moves out and I never see her again?" he questioned.

"That could happen, but is God worth it?" I countered.

"Yes, He is worth it. Okay, I will do it," Glen said, and then he rushed off to get my feeding tube orders.

Having the feeding tube put down my nose and throat was no picnic. It was a painful ordeal and it made my nose bleed and throat hurt. After three attempts, it was finally confirmed in place by an X-ray. Then it was time to try my first feeding. For the trial run, we went light with just two ounces of TwoCal (T-Cal), an extremely high-calorie liquid meal replacement. It contained almost five hundred calories in just eight ounces of liquid. Let the feeding begin. You will never guess what happened...that T-Cal went in easily. I didn't have an issue with gagging on the taste since it was entering through my feeding tube. After about a minute, I thought, "YES!!! Success!!!"

As the T-Cal sat in my stomach for a few minutes,

things started to happen. My tummy rumbled angrily within me, then the entire two ounces came back up. If throwing up without a feeding tube is bad, then throwing up with a feeding tube is horrific! What went wrong? My stomach was not working. It rejected everything that hit it. Solid, liquid, coming in past my lips or through a feeding tube, it didn't matter. My stomach could not digest food, so it simply sent that food back out with a vengeance. I was doomed to suck on ice chips and starve, with my occasional orange slice and banana bag, until my body started working again.

Was it even possible for my body to start working again if it was only getting minimal nourishment? Wouldn't I just continue to starve? How would my organs start working again? I was so far gone that only a miracle could pull me out of death's bed. I had only to lean on God, so that is what I did. The feeding tube was left in place with hopes of having a different reaction over the next few days. We experimented with only one ounce of fluid, and then when that didn't work, we tried just a half-ounce. The results were just as bad, leaving me retching long past the time no more liquid was present.

Things became worse with that awful tube, so I pulled it out myself. That tube was torturing me for no reason. It rubbed my throat raw and caused my oxygen levels to dip, so why leave it in when we couldn't even use it for its intended purpose: nourishment? Why hope to feel satisfied and curb the rat-gnawing hunger pains when it all just came back up and drained me of any energy reserve I had stored?

Even though "my end of the deal" didn't go as planned, my nurse Glen came in for his next shift glowing. He had gone home and talked to his girlfriend. She admitted to him that she had been having second thoughts about their living situation and had also been longing to get closer to the Lord. His end of the deal held up beautifully. They were eventually engaged while living separately and chasing after God. I don't know if they ever married, but I do know that God works in inexplicable ways.

TWENTY-ONE

FREEZING AND FRIENDS

A cheerful heart is good medicine, but a crushed spirit dries up the bones.

PROVERBS 17:22
(NIV)

Guillain-Barré treatments were double edged. Every other day I received a treatment called plasmapheresis and on the opposite days I would receive intravenous immunoglobulin (IVIg). Both treatments were used to aid in stopping my white blood cells from further attacking my nervous system.

Plasmapheresis is the procedure that almost had me transferred to a different hospital. The brand-new machine had been ordered, and I would be the first one to use it. Both wonderful and scary. I didn't really like the idea of being the "pilot patient" on a piece of machinery that would be removing the blood from my body, spinning it to separate the plasma from the rest of my blood, replacing the original plasma with synthetic plasma, and then returning the new blood cocktail loaded with plasma that was not my own back into my body. Kind of crazy having your blood filtered out and then put back in while you watch, but since this was God's answer to our prayers, I trusted that it would be okay.

The IVIg was much less invasive and was a simple three-hour IV drip of immunoglobulin. Each bag of immunoglobulin requires about one thousand blood donors, and each bag of the plasma for the plasmapheresis requires about the same number of plasma donors. So thank you to all of the blood donors out there that helped save my life. It took a lot of you!

I couldn't start the treatments immediately because first I had to have a catheter put into either my pulmonary artery or my femoral artery. As usual, there are risks with these treatments and procedures, so waivers were being thrown at me along every turn. Gratefully, I just nodded to my mom and she was able to sign most of the waivers for me, but when it came to the catheter that would be used in filtering my blood, I was required to sign it myself via the chicken scratch that I now called my own. I also had to choose the catheter location. The risks were huge no matter what I chose. Both locations had the usual infection risks—bleeding out, and other dangers—but the biggest risks were possibly puncturing a lung, heart infection issues with the pulmonary artery location, and paralysis or bleeding to death with the femoral artery location.

I chose the femoral artery. After all, I was already paralyzed and that seemed better than not being able to breathe, or having my heart damaged by an infection on top of my current issues.

My mom was kicked out of my room while the catheter

was inserted. I was completely awake for this and could actually watch! What?!?! I had nowhere better to be and nothing better to do, so I lay there and watched as the surgeon inserted a tube into the femoral artery in my right leg. The major artery that lay between a major nerve and a major vein. This tube thing looked like a large plastic straw about eight inches long and as big around as an ink pen. My eyes popped open with a "no way that's going in my leg" look.

The tiny wisp of a surgeon prepped that area of my leg with all sorts of sterile coverings, cleaners, and potions, each new sensation overwhelming my already raw nervous system. "Okay, hold your breath until I say you can breathe again. You must be completely still. You wouldn't want me to nick your vein or nerve, would you?" stated the surgeon. I was nervous. He adjusted his glasses, bit his lower lip, and got straight to work.

I took as deep a breath as my lungs would allow and tried not to move as I stared wide-eyed at the large straw-like catheter which was being inserted into my leg.

"Oh, good job. The catheter is now in place. I just need to secure it with some stitches and will get out of your way."

Ouch! Did he just put stitches in without numbing the skin on my leg? Yup. Well, that hurt. I still bear the scar of that catheter today. It looks like an upside-down smiley face staring up at me, reminding me it was indeed there and that I did not dream those horrible moments. And, yes, it helped to save my life. That scar is not something to be looked down upon, rather it is there to remind me that I survived. Treatments were able to begin the following day.

A huge box of a machine was wheeled into my room the following afternoon, along with my new contracted techni-cian who, like everyone else thus far, carried a smile on his face. Mr. Technician went through the steps of taking my temperature, sterilizing the catheter area, hooking me up to the machine, connecting the plasma bag, and starting my first treatment of plasmapheresis. After only about thirty seconds of starting the plasmapheresis, I told him I was getting cold even though I was already continually under a pile of blankets due to my lack of body fat and immobility. But this was an abnormal cold; I was cold from the inside out. The longer the procedure lasted, the colder I became, until my teeth were chattering uncontrollably.

"Your lips and fingertips have a bluish tint to them," Mr. Technician remarked. "Could we get some heated blankets in here?" he called to the nurses. The blankets were wrapped around me, kind of like swaddling a baby or preparing a mummy for burial. Although the heated blankets felt good, they did nothing to remove the chill coming from inside my veins. What was going on? Funny stuff that plasma.

Apparently, when plasma is collected, it must be immediately frozen and has a one-year shelf life in that frozen state. It can only be thawed immediately before use, but for some reason mine was being administered as a freezing slushy instead of fully thawed. Barely thawed liquid was being added to my blood and put back into my body, thus I was freezing from the inside out.

Not much thought was given to this by either my mom or me because we didn't know anything about plasma or this procedure, and the technician didn't suggest any changes be made either. My post-treatment temperature had dropped four degrees, down to 93.8 degrees from my normal pre-treatment temperature of 97.8 degrees. Ooh, that was cold! Hypothermic actually.

I warmed up eventually and returned back to "normal."

I thought this was just part of the treatment and didn't think to ask if anything else could be done.

The next day I had my IVIg treatment, which made me overwhelmingly nauseated. I switched off every other day between the two treatments. Freezing cold plasma one day, nauseating IVIg the other. This was not a fun cycle that took up hours of my days.

On day five of my treatments, my mom began pacing the floor and ranting to the technician, "I don't like my daughter freezing to hypothermic levels, even if it is for a short amount of time. Freezing from the inside out does not seem like a good treatment plan. Can't anything be done?"

"The technician had better choose his words carefully— he doesn't know he is dealing with a momma lion on the prowl," I thought.

As he was hooking me up to the machine, he said, "Yeah! I don't know why they deliver it to us partially frozen. They can thaw it just before the procedure."

Wrong words. My mom rounded on that technician and nearly removed his head. Her wrath and fury were full force. "You mean to tell me you knew all along that this stuff didn't have to be frozen? You knew it could be thawed?"

"Yes, ma'am. I've never used cold plasma on a patient before."

"So you've just been letting her freeze? You could have killed her! Are you crazy? How can we thaw this stuff out?"

"Just run the bag under some hot water and squish it around so there are no hot spots. You can't microwave it, but it can be set out an hour or two before treatment begins. I don't have time to let it thaw once I get here; the hospital I usually work at is over an hour away. I come here just for your daughter."

My mom rushed the bag over to the sink in my room

and squished it under the hot running water as long as she could until Mr. Technician needed it. I felt sorry for the technician that day, but my treatments were much better going forward. That day I reached teeth-chattering levels of cold because we only had time to run the bag under hot water for a few minutes before it was needed. Needless to say, it was fully thawed and room temperature for the rest of my remaining cycles.

Looking back on this situation, I can see some humor in it all. There I was, lying wrapped up like a mummy in heated blankets with only my face showing, my teeth chattering wildly, and my lips turning blue. It must have been a sight. Also, after my surprise birthday party, the word had spread that I was very ill and in the hospital, so visitors began flooding in at all times of the day. During one of my freezing plasmapheresis mummy-wrapped episodes, my boyfriend's parents dropped by for a visit but could only stand outside my room and wave at me from the window.

I can't even imagine what they were thinking seeing me bundled up like that, shaking violently while my blood was being removed and replaced. I'm sure they wondered why their son was sticking around. I sure wondered why he stuck around.

By this time, Wayne was back at the University of Texas, in Austin. He went to school and worked about two and a half hours away from our hometown, where I was currently located in ICU, so between school, work, and studies he was only able to drive in on the weekends. And drive he did. Every weekend he didn't have to study for a major test, he drove in and sat beside my hospital bed. He just sat there and held my hand.

The first weekend he came to the hospital, I attempted to talk with him, "You know you don't have to come here. I don't know if I will recover or die. I might never be able to walk again or live a normal life. I might have lifelong obstacles."

"Shh. Shh. It's okay. You don't need to talk. I know it's hard and hurts your throat. I can't even understand what you are saying anyway," he replied in as soothing a voice as he could muster, all with a huge smile shining on his face.

"Listen, I don't want you to be scarred for life if I die! You need to just move on with your life. Forget about me," I declared, in a whispered voice.

"I'm not going anywhere." He smiled at me. After a few minutes, he got up, walked into the hallway, and wept with my mom. I never saw him cry. I never saw him crack or look down or depressed. He allowed himself that one moment of release, then he came back beside my bed and held my hand. Each weekend he returned again and again and again.

Visitors became a sustaining part of my recovery. In those long days at the hospital, I was actually deteriorating even further and was worse off than when I was first admitted.

The first two nights, my mom slept in the ICU with me. She was in this uncomfortable, green vinyl, recliner bed/chair thing. There was no way that thing was comfortable but, somehow, she would manage to pass out while I would lie awake. After she was out cold, it would only take a few minutes for her to begin snoring and I would stare at her in the semi-darkness, wishing I could sleep like her. On the third night, it was too much. She looked awful. I'm not even sure she had been home once since I had been admitted, which is understandable after the horrors we encountered at the other hospital. But I felt safe at this hospital. The nurses kept vigil over me, the candy stripers were in to take my blood every three hours, I had a lung capacity breathing test every three hours (not on the same rotation as the blood draws), and a lung X-ray each night, so I was pretty much never alone, or asleep.

On the third night, my mom leaned back, fell asleep, and began snoring out her night song. Due to her exhaustion, each minute that ticked past brought louder and louder snores. Finally, I simply could not take it any longer. I began yelling for her to wake up, but since my yell was nothing more than a halting whisper, she didn't even stir.

I somehow willed my hand to pick something up and throw it at her. Needless to say, the soft object I threw didn't even clear my bed, and her snores just grew louder. One of the side effects of Guillain-Barré is a racing heart rate, so as I became more and more anxious in my endeavors to wake my mom, my heart rate began to skyrocket to nearly two hundred bpm. It crept so high that I triggered alarms at the nurses' station, and they came running to see what was wrong.

"What's wrong? Are you all right? I thought you were going into cardiac arrest!" yell-whispered one of the nurses. "Well, what's wrong?"

"She. Is. Snoring. I can't get any rest!" I pointed to my mom and the nurse chuckled out loud. She gently woke my mom up. "Honey, I think you should just go on home and get a good night's sleep," she cooed to my mom.

"Please, Mom! I can't relax like this. Please go home. You won't be any good to either of us until you take care of yourself." It took some convincing from me that I wanted her to go, but I think she may have been relived when I ordered her out of my room that night, and on several other nights to come.

The next morning at around 7:30 a.m., I had a visitor.

This may not seem like a big deal, but it was for my mom. The night before, she had promised me that she would be back at 7:30 a.m. but, somehow, she was actually able to sleep, freshen up, and do a few things she needed to do. She was worried about not being back at the hospital when she had promised to be, and prayed that God would keep me safe without her.

God had known that my mom would need the extra time, so He sent me a visitor named Louise Graves instead. Louise stayed, laughed, prayed, and told me stories until my mom was able to arrive. Mostly we talked about the return of the Lord, and what we thought heaven would look like. This woman was a powerhouse for the Lord, and her conversation filled me with peace and joy. It touched my mom's heart to know that God answered even that simple prayer of companionship for me when she was absent. And I had the honor of returning the favor and visiting Louise in the hospital when she was sick a few years later.

Hospital visitors are a funny thing. Each of them has a style all their own. Some just come quickly, to drop by hospital survival needs like magazines and outside food, and others come and stay awhile. Some are terrified of hospitals and seem hesitant to be there at all. They just stand in one spot, switching their body weight from one leg to the other until they can escape. Others come because it is the ministry God has called them to. No matter the visitor, they are all needed and welcome to the lonely and weary person on their sick bed.

One of my most memorable visitors was my best friend's mom, who also happened to be my mom's best friend. She is small in stature but big in personality. And the Energizer Bunny has nothing on her. This woman is in constant motion and talks just as fast.

One afternoon, she stopped by for a visit and sat down in a chair next to my bed closest to the door. My mom was in a chair on the other side of my bed by the window. Immediately, our friend began to talk and tell us all about everything that was on her mind. She jumped from thought to thought, all while gesturing with her hands and nodding her head vigorously.

My eyes were having trouble keeping up with all of her movement due to the double and triple vision I endured, so my heart rate began to climb. Slowly at first, but I was unaware of how high it actually raced until three nurses came running into my room ready to shock me back to life. Apparently, my heart rate had risen higher than they had ever experienced before, and they were ready to deal with a crashing patient. But nope, I was just lying there in my bed listening to our very lively family friend.

The nurses politely yet convincingly asked her to leave so I could rest and not have my heart explode. She quite easily obeyed, only to return and repeat another day. I looked forward to her visits that brought moments of normalcy into the room.

My dad's friends were the most curious visitors. Many of his friends came to visit me over the days, and usually they made themselves comfortable and stayed awhile. What I found odd was that almost all of them had to open the wardrobe in my room to see what was inside. First of all, why does an ICU room need a wardrobe? Patients are very ill and possibly dying, it's not like we are getting up and trying on clothes to look cute for our friends. My wardrobe sat empty. And it was imperative that the doors stayed shut. The wardrobe was against the wall at the foot of my bed, under the wall-mounted television. If it was left open, my eyes were unable to focus properly, due to the natural wood grain pattern in the doors. When the grain pattern didn't match up due to the doors being left open, it would leave me feeling nauseated because of the double and triple vision I suffered. Yet, each of my dad's friends just had to open that wardrobe and look inside. And being that they were men, they almost never shut the doors properly.

Then they would sit down in a chair by my bed, usually on the side near the window, grab the television remote, turn the TV on, and switch it to a golf channel. They were kind enough to keep the volume low, thank God, because noise also bothered me. My room probably sounded like a tomb due to how quiet I kept it. Other than the noises in the hallway and my beeping machines, I could barely tolerate any extra sound. Anyway, they would settle in for the long haul, sit and watch sports next to my bed for an hour or two, tell me a few crazy stories from their younger years, pray over me, then leave.

Only a few times did they actually show up when my dad was there, and then I would just listen to my dad and his friends talk to each other. Oh, the stories they told. It was extremely entertaining. Looking back, I wish I had a recording of all their stories. It was always comforting hearing the strong masculine voices tell stories of their youth even if I did just lie there with my eyes closed, listening.

I had many family members and friends visit me, both young and old, bearing gifts. My favorite was a gift from Susan, a lady that I knew from both church and school. Susan made the best and most beautiful homemade cookies. One day she came to the hospital with an entire box of her famous cookies, intricately decorated just for me. There were hearts, butterflies, and flowers that I knew tasted every bit as wonderful as they looked.

My mom oohed and aahed over them for the longest time, and then set the entire box in my lap for me to admire. I loved those cookies and the lady that made them. I couldn't eat them, but they touched my heart as deeply as a good meal would have touched my stomach. They were nourishment for the soul. The thought and effort put into them was overwhelming. My mom froze that entire box of cookies for me to eat when I was recovered. Another incentive for me to hang in there.

TWENTY-TWO

BLIND

Just then a woman who had been subject to bleeding for twelve years came up behind Jesus and touched the edge of His cloak. She said to herself, "If I only touch his cloak, I will be healed." Jesus turned and saw her. "Take heart, daughter," he said, "your faith has healed you." And the woman was healed at that moment.

MATTHEW 9:20-22
(NIV)

I n the midst of all the visitors, my treatments continued and my condition worsened. I became weaker by the day and was eventually unable to even lift my head up off the pillow for the briefest of moments. Between visitors, my mom and I had many quiet times where she would just sit and read the Bible. In one such quiet time, I remember looking at her and saying, "After all this, I can have twins with no painkiller, no problem." I have no idea where that thought came from, but maybe it was God preparing me for a future. My future.

Up until that point, I never alluded to a life after Guillain-Barré. I was too weary to think beyond the present moment, but in the midst of all the pain and suffering, a moment of life sprung out of my lips and I declared birth without the worry of pain. Even in this weakened state, I had a glimmer of hope for a life beyond Guillain-Barré. And, I had somehow prophesied over myself. Not in the having twins, but in giving birth with no painkiller. I went on years later to have homebirths, with a midwife, to three precious babies, all with the doctors' golden seal of approval. The doctors didn't want to ever see me in a hospital again!

After this statement, my two favorite nurses—Glen and Kathy—came in to weigh me again. I was simply unable to help them, so they had to scoop me off the bed to zero out the scale and then placed me back on to register my weight. I was down to a horrifyingly low weight of seventy-two pounds. They couldn't believe the reading, so they weighed me two more times, each one saying the same number. They hung their heads and Glen cried.

"I will never weigh you again!" Glen cried. "As far as I am concerned, weighing bones doesn't count."

Later that day, my much-loved nun stopped by to pray. I am not Catholic and have had little experience with nuns in my life, but this nun has my utmost love and respect. She was a little, old, gray-haired lady that wore a large cross on a chain around her neck, along with her black habit without a head covering.

Every time she visited, she would shuffle into my room and slowly walk up to the side of my bed, take my hand, and ask permission to pray. She looked so small and frail, yet when she opened her mouth a giant of a woman came out. I'm sure if I could have seen into the spiritual realm when she prayed, I would have seen a mighty warrior dressed in full armor doing battle on behalf of the one for whom she was praying. Her words were always slow, soft, gentle and intentional, but the power behind them was like a flaming sword. On her every visit, she continually brought me to cleansing tears, and I agreed with every word uttered from her lips.

One day, after she left, time continued on slowly and quietly. Time was not only grating on me, but also on my parents. It was one of those never-ending days where you prayed for night to arrive. Night did finally arrive, to the disillusioned weariness of us all.

I kicked my parents out of my hospital room. Not out of anger, but out of love. They had been taking turns curling up in the little green vinyl ICU hospital chair by my bed, only to wake up more exhausted the next day than they had been the night before. I knew they would go crazy with sleep deprivation, so I made them go home and ordered them to not return until they had slept, showered, and eaten. I assured them I would be fine; after all, the nurses checked on me all night long. And if I died...that was okay too. No, I didn't tell them it was okay if I died that night— they wouldn't have left if I did—but, seriously, after everything I had been through, I was so ready to go home; to Heaven. Little did I know that THAT night would be one of the worst, and one of the best, nights of my illness. God met me in my room that night.

Sleep eludes those in extreme pain. It comes in short spurts, more like passing out and coming to. This night I actually slept and the nurses did not wake me up. They came by my room throughout the night to take my blood, measure my lung capacity, do a chest X-ray, but when they saw that I was actually sleeping, they had mercy on me and let me rest.

It was relatively quiet for an ICU, which is always bustling with activity, tests, and emergencies. When I finally did startle awake in the middle of the night, as I so often did, I immediately knew that this time something was different. An ICU is never dark. There are always bright lights in the hall, casting their glow around the window blinds, and dim lights in the patients' rooms. The machines cast strange blinking lights on the walls and ceiling, along with the beeping and whirring sounds that inform anyone within range that they are doing their jobs.

Shadows ink across the ceiling without invitation, and shoes squeak on the floor in the hallway outside as the nurses make their rounds. A nightlight is never necessary in the ICU. But this night, when I opened my eyes during the wee hours of darkness, I realized that something was off. Something was wrong. Yes, everything was wrong; I was dying after all. My organs and body were shutting down on me, paralyzed and unable to make my limbs respond to the easiest of tasks, but this was different; this was worse. I heard the beeping of my machines and looked in their direction. Nothing. I glanced toward the window where I knew the bright lights from the nurses' station glared incessantly, even when I was trying to sleep. Nothing. I scoured the expanse before me, yet not a glimmer of light pierced my eyes. I could not see. I was blind.

This time my limbs did what I asked. Just as my mind willed it, my hand reached out into the darkness to grasp... what? I'm not sure what I was reaching for. My heart was calling out to Jesus and my body responded by stretching out my hand and arm into the air before me. But then, the unexpected happened. Something, someone, grasped my hand and held on tight. An angelic Latin voice spoke to me in a deep slow rhythm, that sounded like a rich gentle lullaby, that could rock me into a sweet and endless sleep. "Hello, Natalie, my name is Angel and I have come to pray with you."

My breath gasped out of me in pure anguish when I realized I was not alone. Somehow, I was able to eek out the words, "I'm blind. I can't see." Tears began to stream down my face in silent tracks of pain. No sobs broke forth from my chest, but my tears told the truth of my deep distress better than any feeble words ever could.

We connected in that moment, Angel and I. His pure love poured over me and I knew—KNEW—that I was not alone. Yes, I knew that God was always with me, but this timing, this voice, this personal lullaby that was so tender and full of compassion told me that GOD WAS WITH ME, even at my very lowest of lows.

I had always feared blindness. Even as a child I knew that I never wanted to go blind. The thought of navigating this world in darkness was scary. Even with that trace of apprehension living inside of me, I never gave blindness more than a passing thought. I didn't think loss of sight was anything I would personally experience. Even with everything going wrong with my body due to Guillain-Barré, I never expected to open my eyes to complete darkness, being swallowed by a void so black it seemed to press against me on every side. This darkness was thick and heavy, like a weighted blanket trying to smother out my very existence.

Angel prayed for me. His voice was like a musical ballad written just for me, nourishing and fixing a deep part of my soul that had withered. His prayer of worship was a weapon that broke the back of fear and allowed a warrior to rise up in its place. In the dark of night and blindness, he prayed and gripped my hand like an anchor, steadying me for the remainder of my fight ahead. His prayers tickled my ears while my tears ran in rivulets, soaking the pillow under my head.

After a long and gentle silence, Angel released my hand and tucked me in. I rolled over with a renewed sense of hope and a peace that passes all understanding. I fell into a gentle sleep and awoke the next morning able to see again.

Fear had been vanquished, and my master's hands had touched both my eyes and my heart. I could see the light of day again.

TWENTY-THREE

POWER

Jesus knew what they were thinking and asked,
"Why are you thinking these things in your hearts?
Which is easier: to say, 'Your sins are forgiven,' or to
say, 'Get up and walk'? But I want you to know that
the Son of Man has authority on earth to forgive
sins." So he said to the paralyzed man, "I tell you, get
up, take your mat and go home." Immediately he
stood up in front of them, took what he had been
lying on and went home praising God.

LUKE 5:22-25
(NIV)

After having my sight restored, my body began to crash. I was vomiting anytime I sucked on ice chips and sometimes for no reason at all. Not much came up, just stomach acid, but it still made me choke, so the nurses strapped me to my bed and turned it into a bed chair. Basically, they made the foot of the bed point down and the head of the bed point up with the middle of the bed staying horizontal. Since I was unable to hold myself up or stay in the bed with my own strength, they strapped me to it. I sat there, strapped to my bed in a sitting position, with my head hanging down, chin on my chest, as limp as a rag doll. I had officially hit my absolute lowest physical point.

I'm sure my weight had plummeted even further, but without being weighed there was no telling how low it was. My fight had been drained.

I was alone that day. My parents were out doing some of the neglected and much-needed things to keep our family's existence going, and I hadn't had any visitors. I was glad to be alone. I wasn't strong enough for anything other than solitude. Even though, at just the right time, God did send someone to see me that afternoon—my pastor, Gary Kerr. He had visited me in the hospital multiple times before. His first visit was on the day I was finally admitted to the hospital, and he had been a few times thereafter with my church's youth pastor and worship leaders. But today he was alone.

As I sat there, weak and limp, I heard my ICU room door open and close. I opened my left eye from within my hanging head to peek at who had walked into my room. I saw him take one look at me and watched as his own head hung in miserable defeat. I closed my eye again and simply dangled there. I heard his shoes squeak on the floor as he tentatively plodded over to my bed. I listened as he sighed a deep and heavy breath. I guessed that seeing the state I was in was hard on him, something like a sucker punch to the gut.

His prayer in that moment was so honest. So vulnerable. So sincere. He took out his anointing oil, put it on his finger and said, "Lord, I don't even know what to pray, but would you just heal her?"

He anointed my forehead with that oil and POWER shot through my body like an electrified bolt of lightning. It wasn't hot or painful, but more like a strong, tingling cleansing with strength like a raging river behind it, yet controlled and purposeful.

I didn't move and didn't flinch, so my pastor probably had no idea what I had just experienced. He stood there another moment longer, taking in shallow breaths, then let me be, squeaking his way back out the door.

But I felt that power. Like nothing I had ever felt before. It was life, healing, love, and hope all rolled up in one. I KNEW that I was healed. And that my healing would be manifested.

When the world looks at you and says, "It is over," that is when God steps in to say, "It is NOT over."

Something had begun in the heavenlies. Something had begun in my body. No formula, no warrior prayer, no giant of faith and praise. That simple, desperate, heartfelt prayer from a godly man collided with all the prayers that had come before, and my healing that had been paid for through Jesus' stripes two thousand years before began to manifest.

I felt the same and I looked the same, but I knew that from that day forward, I would never be the same. One day I would walk completely free. No, the battle was not over, but my heart and mind were officially fortified that I would most certainly be fully healed and pain-free in the time to come. I felt that power and needed to walk it out.

It was time for the struggle of breaking free from the stifling cocoon called Guillain-Barré.

———

I f you couldn't tell from how weak I had become, I should tell you that I had practically stopped talking. My body needed all of its energy, so the simple things like lifting my head, moving, and talking were out of the question. I spent most of my days just lying still, either listing to my mom read the Bible, hearing visitors come and go, or talking to God myself inside of my own head. Since I was no longer speaking, I hadn't told my parents about the visit from Angel or the POWERful prayer from my pastor.

Even after POWERful healing began, I had to climb back from this valley to rise up. At night my body had begun doing its own thing. Strange things. Maybe these were just the symptoms of the manifestation of the healing that had begun, but they sure felt sci-fi to me.

The few times I did fall asleep, I woke up with something on my face. The first time it happened it scared me. I will never forget the sensation. It was like a large spider, only heavy and fleshy instead of hairy.

When my brain told my hand to swipe the mystery object away from my face, the object squeezed. My face was being gently squeezed by this mysterious spider! "What is this thing? What is it doing to me, and why is it on my face?" I thought.

Oh wait!?!? Hmm, mystery solved. It was my hand. My hand was on my face and was unsympathetic to my brain's instructions. My brain said "swipe off man-eating spider" and my hand said "squeeze sweet face." I wanted to laugh when I realized that my hand was actually the large fleshy spider, but laughing would have been too much work, so instead I lay there trying to figure out how to get said hand off my face. This began happening to me regularly. I would wake up with my hand on my face, then my fingers would wiggle and squeeze while my brain attempted to tell it to move.

Eventually, my hand did listen and move accordingly, but this ritual became a familiar part of my dark hours. Not only that, but I decided it was high time I set some goals for myself. After all, I was going to experience complete healing.

My first goal was to wiggle my toes. I hadn't had any type of control over my legs and feet in quite some time, so this seemed enormous. Upon admission to the hospital, they strapped air compression sleeves on my legs to keep my blood flowing. They were hot, sticky, and very uncomfortable. Every few moments they would fill with air, making a ratcheting noise, then they would whoosh all the air out like a bicycle pump and start over again. Day and night. I am amazed I can even look at an air pump today because those leg compressors drove me crazy. Not only did they feel irritating to my legs and their sound grate on my ears, but I also had a very strange sensation that would come and go from that general direction.

Off and on, I would feel like either my toes or my legs were extremely heavy, like anchors were strapped to them, and at the same time they felt like they were crossed. I would ask my mom over and over to see if my toes were crossed and to please uncross them.

I made this same complaint to my pastor's wife, Lori, and also to the massage therapist friend of mine, Joanna.

Lori took the opportunity to tell me a funny story about feeling like her legs were crossed when she had an epidural, and Joanna decided that my toes needed to be rubbed, rolled, and loved on by her anointed hands. Both the epidural story and the massage were great, but neither could convince me that my toes, or sometimes my legs, were not crossed.

I remember the first time I consciously wiggled my big toe. I had set this goal to wiggle my toes, so each day I would sit there staring at my toes, commanding them to move with my mind. One day I couldn't believe it—I told my toe to move and it did! No big movements, but it responded when I asked it to. A tiny, almost imperceptible, movement of my big toe. I felt like I had won the Nobel Peace Prize. It felt so good. I had been trying to wiggle my toes for days and now it had happened! I am sure my lack of facial expression belied how I felt inside, but I was so excited to have my body respond properly when my brain requested it to.

Even through the bizarre behaviors and utter flaws of my body, God would have it that I began to heal. I started to gain strength. I began to move again, and slowly even talk again. I still wasn't eating, so nourishment was not my miracle. God was.

Eventually, I was able to make all of my body parts respond properly and do what I wanted them to do. My body was difficult, weak, and messy, but it responded. Great news! Now I get to have a physical therapist. Huh?!?!? I was so not expecting that. At least not yet. I was tired and felt like I needed to recover from a marathon, or my death bed, before starting therapy but, apparently, the longer I didn't use my muscles and movement, the less likely I was to gain them back. So therapy it was.

The doctors sent a physical therapist to my hospital room. He was young and physically very strong. His muscles were huge, while my muscles were...well, they weren't. I had once been a runner and cheerleader who prided herself on physical fitness. I lost it all. I looked like a holocaust refugee, so I'm not sure I still had muscles. Okay, yes, I did still have them, but they had atrophied so much that they were unrecognizable as muscle. A more accurate description would have been mush instead of muscle.

The first day my therapy was underwhelming as the therapist had me sit on the side of my bed. Yup. My task, should I choose to accept it, was to sit. I had to try and pull myself up to a sitting position, throw my legs over the edge of the bed, and not fall off of Mount St. Bed O' Covers. That's what it felt like. Who knew therapy for sitting on the side of the bed could be so difficult? I had several attempts at doing it. It felt like an hour of attempts before I was finally able to pull myself up to sitting without any help, and two hours of attempts before I could swing my legs over the side without having Therapy Man catch me as I tumbled to the ground.

Do you know how humbling it is for a twenty-year-old woman with greasy bun hair, acne, floating crossed eyes, and no muscles being caught over and over again by Mr. Muscles as he moves my catheter tube out of the way? All in an open tie-back hospital gown? Nope? I didn't think so!

Mr. Muscles returned every single day. I couldn't catch a break. Before long he had me pushing myself up to sitting all on my own, so we moved on to knuckle push-ups! Hard-core training! Okay, not really. He stood me up facing the wall (I wore pajama pants under my hospital gown for this session...I did have some propriety) where I did wall knuckle push-ups. This was basically me standing, facing the wall, being held at the waist by Mr. Muscles, and bending my elbows a few times before being worn out for the next several hours.

A few days later, Mr. Muscles had me walking. Or, more accurately, he carried me down the hospital halls using a walker. Along with leg exercises that I could do while lying in bed to gain strength AND to lose those dreaded leg compressors. I would say that my physical therapy was shaping up just fine.

I seemed to be moving fairly quickly in my road to recovery, especially for someone that didn't eat. My strength was returning and that nauseating double and triple vision was gone after being blind! So, the next logical step, according to my doctors, was to remove the catheter and have me pee on my own, then send me home to recover. Well, sort of. Not before going to an inpatient physical therapy hospital.

TWENTY-FOUR

OUTPATIENT PLEASE

The Sovereign Lord is my strength! He makes me as surefooted as a deer, able to tread upon the heights.

HABAKKUK 3:19
(NLT)

After being released from ICU with a bottle of morphine, a box of morphine patches, a prescription for arthritis, and several other "necessities," my parents took me to the inpatient therapy hospital; the place that would be my home for the next six weeks or more.

There was an entire process we had to follow to get a gold card and some other stuff before being admitted, but I think I have blocked most of that out of my memory. I do remember that at the same time I registered for my gold card, I also tried to get social security and was denied. The doctor looked at me with an ugly sneer on his face, and as I sat mostly paralyzed in my wheelchair, unable to hold my own head up, he said, "Go get a job. You are denied." The unpleasant process included visiting unsavory parts of town and sitting uncomfortably in a rickety wheelchair for long hours, waiting on paperwork and approval. Once I was approved for the gold card, but denied social security, I was allowed to tour my new home.

NO, NO, NO, NO, NO!

The inpatient therapy hospital was a place nightmares were made of. A place where underpaid and underprivileged government-assigned therapists preyed on the innocent and defenseless patients.

It was in a very old and dark brick building with the windows painted black and was located on the opposite side of town from where my family lived. Another drawback was that it was surrounded by heavy traffic. The building was dirty and falling apart with dust and grime covering almost every surface. Shoes stuck to the floor and made a sticky ripping sound when a person walked down the halls. Visitors were only allowed on two specific days a week for a few short hours. I felt like the short visiting hours were a ploy to keep prying eyes out.

Not one single person smiled even once while we were there. No patients smiled. Most of them looked like they were waiting to die or commit suicide, their eyes downcast and seized with fear. Many of them were in wheelchairs, like me, and many more were confined to their beds. No nurses smiled. They looked like they should be in a therapy hospital themselves just counting down to when they may emotionally erupt. I even heard a few nurses yelling and cursing at patients behind closed doors.

Not only was there a lingering spirit of hopelessness in that place, but it also smelled of death. I'm not sure if it was a physical smell I noticed, or the spiritual stench of the place that I was picking up. The hallways cast an eerie, dark yellow glow, and it seemed shadows lurked everywhere; not a single room was lit to full viewing capacity. It felt like a place where unspeakable horrors took place behind closed doors at night.

I knew that I could not stay there. I thought I would be abused, raped, or even killed simply by neglect or on purpose. Fear grasped throats with its inky black fingers and choked the life out of the people there; I know because I could feel the oppression dragging me down, and I was only taking a tour.

One patient begged for me to help him escape. He wasn't really able to speak properly as half of his face drooped, so he whispered in quick, slurred words. He was a gunshot wound survivor. His head was wrapped in gauze and he trolled the halls in a wheelchair by pulling himself around with his one good leg. He managed to get all the way to the elevator while I was there but was caught by an angry nurse who grudgingly wheeled him back to his room. He cried for help all the way back while trying to stop his chair from moving forward by dragging his foot on the ground, but he was no match for the husky nurse behind him.

A second patient insisted that he was being beaten every night when his medicine was brought to him. Another nurse intercepted him and told me not to listen to him because he was being approved for psychiatric meds soon. She said he was crazy but, looking back, I'm not so sure he was.

When the tour was over and we had climbed back into my dad's truck, I was emphatic that I simply could not and would not stay there. I would just have to do therapy on my own at home. In my mind there was no other option.

We prayed and asked the Lord to open another door, and He did. There happened to be a brand-new outpatient therapy clinic just down the street from where we lived. The price tag wasn't pretty, but the place was pristine. It required my mom taking me to various therapy sessions several times a week. I was signed up for physical therapy to relearn everyday skills like balance and walking; speech therapy to relearn how to speak and use my vocal cords; and occupational therapy to regain those fine motor skills needed to brush my teeth, eat, write, dress myself, and all those other things we take for granted when healthy. Those sessions coupled with me working hard at home, with my mom's help, made me feel like I really could plug into God's power and be fully healed again. This place was clean, well lit, and had state-of-the-art therapy equipment. And to top it all off...Mr. Muscles worked there.

I was going to bust out of this cocoon after all! When can we start?

However, physical therapy was no picnic. I was given a list of exercises to complete at home, and they all seemed impossible to me. I had to use those colored exercise bands and work up from the lightest one to the strongest one. Simple things like hamstring stretches and quadriceps stretches while lying on my back and stomach, then applying resistance against the colored band of choice, seemed impossible.

Wow! It was so difficult. Stretching was agonizing after lying still for so long. I had lost all the elasticity and flexibility earned as an athlete, and my muscles had become as tight as a guitar from disuse and those dreaded charley horses I had endured. I also began doing leg lifts. Buns of steel, here we come! Maybe not quite buns of steel because I could only lift my leg an inch or two at a time, but it was progress. Stretching, exercising, no more double and triple vision, no more charley horses, and my body was doing what I asked it to do. Sure, I was still experiencing crazy pain, tingling nerves, and could still only eat oranges, but this was sweet relief. I was finally working toward healing.

My first outpatient therapy session included balance skills and walking. I had lost all of my reflexes from Guillain-Barré, so I literally could have been knocked over with a feather. Weighing seventy-five-ish pounds was not much help but, yes, I had gained weight by eating only a few oranges. That's a God thing too.

Mr. Muscles had me stand between parallel bars, then he half carried me back and forth between them several times, trying to get my feet and legs used to the sensation of bearing weight on them again. I dragged and dropped my feet sloppily along because my calf muscles and feet were still mostly paralyzed. I could not push up on my toes and that is part of walking. I couldn't do that, so I had to learn to walk a different way, and it was ugly. Once I was thoroughly worn out, it was time for my balance test.

I was placed in the middle of some gymnastic mats and told to stand still with my feet together but not touching; basically, a neutral standing position. Then I was told to close my eyes while I stood there to see how long I could balance. Whoa! Talk about the world pitching under your feet. The moment I shut my eyes, the world tipped, and I fell straight backwards. Not to fear, Mr. Muscles was there to catch me. It was like playing that falling trust game, only I wasn't trying to fall. In fact, I thought I was standing. I didn't even know I had fallen until strong arms wrapped around me and stood me back up. I did feel the world tip and pitch under me, but I thought I was doing a remarkable job hanging in there, standing straight and tall. Boy, was I wrong. Fall, fall, fall. I had to do this balancing act over and over again until I could stand for several seconds straight with my eyes closed. Each session we worked on this, until I no longer fell and was truly balancing on my own two feet.

TWENTY-FIVE

HOME AND HUNGRY

The spirit of the Lord God is upon me, because the Lord has anointed me to preach good tidings to the poor; He has sent me to heal the brokenhearted, to proclaim liberty to the captives, and the opening of the prison to those who are bound; to proclaim the acceptable year of the Lord, and the day of vengeance of our God; to comfort all who mourn, to console those who mourn in Zion, to give them beauty for ashes, the oil of joy for mourning, the garment of praise for the spirit of heaviness; that they may be called trees of righteousness, the planting of the Lord, that He may be glorified.

ISAIAH 61:1-3
(NKJV)

At home in my own bed, I was doing rehab and gaining strength. And boy, did it feel good to be going to church again! My parents wheeled me in on any Sunday morning that I felt I could make it. I remember one Sunday, when a sweet friend of mine went up for prayer. She had been born with severe physical issues and I asked my parents to wheel me up so I could pray for her. Through my illness, I felt even more connected to her after experiencing some of the things she had gone through since birth. Little did I know that praying for her in church would impact my life not too long in the future.

My whole little church community of Faith West rallied around my family and pitched in wherever they could. One such friend, Elaine, was a nurse who came over multiple times to give me my B-12 shots. My mom was supposed to be giving them to me, but each time she was about to stab me, she would hesitate. Nurse Elaine to the rescue. She was kind and patient teaching my mom what to do and it never hurt when Elaine did, in fact, stab me. Those B-12 shots were supposed to give me a surge of energy, and I took them for quite some time.

During one of my neurology appointments, I complained, "Dr. Diaz, every time I get a B-12 shot, I crash into total exhaustion. When is this energy supposed to kick in?"

"Hmm? Well, for some people they don't work and do the opposite of what they are supposed to do. No more B-12 shots for you! Now you will drink energy drinks. Up to five of them each day if you need."

"Umm, that's a lot of caffeine!" I stated.

"Yes, but you need it for now."

I didn't know any better way to gain energy, so down the hatch they went, just a half a can daily at first, but over time I drank up to two a day. I consumed them just to have enough energy to get through each day without sleeping my life away. Knowing what I know now about energy drinks, I wish I had never drunk them, but at the time they were a lifesaver.

After a while on my new routine, I seemed to be doing so much better. I started to feel semi-human again instead of like a motionless baby wrapped in a tight blanket and encased in pain. I even felt good enough to start drying out and saving the seeds of many of the flowers from the bouquets our family and friends had sent to me. It was therapeutic and very relaxing being surrounded by the scent of flowers and separating out the part of them that is used to spring up new life. My hope was to one day use those seeds to plant a wildflower garden of remembrance. That never did happen, but the memory of those seeds is planted deep in my soul today.

At first glance it seemed I was doing better. With my energy drinks, exercises, morphine patches and pills, flower therapy, and so much more, I was recovering. Until one evening I crashed.

I was still only eating oranges, so I am sure that didn't help my situation out much.

My organs began shutting down and I began convulsing again. "I'm dying," I cried. "I'm not going to make it if we don't get help now."

My parents made the familiar mad dash to the ER, only this time I was immediately admitted into ICU under the care of my neurologist.

Once stabilized, I fell asleep wondering if I was relapsing and thinking that I didn't want to lose all the progress I had made. I couldn't bear the thought of starting over with the pain and complete paralysis. I prayed and hoped that this time would be different. With a yawn and tired eyes, I slowly drifted asleep in the arms of Christ. "I will wait until morning to have my questions answered. I simply cannot think any longer," I thought.

Morning came with bright sunshine and lots of noise. I felt pale and green as if death itself had wrestled with me through the night. That didn't seem to matter to the world around me, for it was all abuzz with schedules and business. As I thought about how loud and energetic life was, as it continued to live on around me, a tall, boisterous doctor burst into my room with a huge smile on his face.

"Today is a wonderful day!" he very loudly proclaimed, all while throwing his arms around and gesturing wildly with his hands as if they held the key to this day's emotions. "I am your neurologist's partner, Dr. Rossi, and a neurologist myself. It is such a wonderful day. Guess what I am going to do for you? I am going to take you off all of your medications!"

"What?" I stammered, thinking I must not have heard him correctly.

"I am taking you off all of your medications. What, do I not speak so clearly with my accent? I am very good looking, you know."

"All...of them?" I asked haltingly.

"Yes, all of them. Especially those pain medications! You don't need them any longer!" Dr. Rossi exclaimed.

Questioning thoughts raced through my mind: "You are so not serious!!! Why would you do a crazy thing like that? I have been in tremendous pain since day one of this thing. I am on morphine patches AND morphine pills. I am on arthritis medication. I am still in tremendous pain. What on earth will I have to endure without those medications? Can I even bear it? Will I survive?"

Animated and loving Dr. Rossi read my mind as each

emotion passed across my face and he answered all my questions.

"You, my dear, are not relapsing!"

"Not relapsing? Then what on earth is going on? I see you reading my mind. Why is he staring at me with that twinkle in his eye? He looks like he has a big secret."

"Yes, you are not relapsing. Good news, yes? You simply had a drug overdose!"

I jolted, my eyes as big as saucers. Thoughts flooded through my mind. Then, when the shock wore off, I said, "A drug overdose? How could that be? I followed all the prescription instructions. I've done everything correctly. I never took too much or abused those drugs. And now you are telling me I had a drug overdose?"

Hands flying, the doctor laughed. "Yes, yes. A drug overdose. Your body is very tiny and is simply done with medications. You can handle no more. I remove you from everything. You will see, you be better soon."

EVERYTHING! All arthritis medication, morphine pills, pain patches, sleeping pills, and a slew of other drugs they had me on. No weaning off. No helping my pain...just full stop.

"Your new treatment is to try to eat. Food. Real food. Go home. Eat. Exercise. Eat some more. Preferably something with a lot of fat in it. Rest and eat again," declared the good doctor.

So I stayed in the hospital a few more days, this time recovering from a drug overdose. The good news was that this had nothing to do with Guillain-Barré...I was still healing.

Guess what? My pain level never changed! Not even when they removed all those medications cold turkey. I didn't feel worse. I never once craved those medications either. I had not become addicted like the professionals feared may happen. Actually, I felt better. My skin no longer had an ash green tint to it, and the nausea that had plagued me slowly began to lift.

After staying in the ICU, I was transferred to a regular room for the last night. During the last day, I was in my room waiting for the release orders with my mom, when I realized I hadn't told her about the night I went blind and was visited by Angel. Even as I recounted the events to my mom, I was not able to confirm if Angel was indeed a man or an angel. I simply did not know. I hadn't seen him with my own eyes. I simply felt him through his anchor of love and heard his pleasing voice.

Who do you then think walked through my door? Angel! He was real.

That melodic Latin voice pierced through the air, "I heard you were going home, and I need to tell you to get all better."

I croaked out in my shaky voice, "Thank you, Angel. Thank you so very much. You will never know how much your middle-of-the-night visit touched me."

"I wanted to come to say goodbye. I will be praying for you. You will not be back," he said.

He smiled and left as his departing prophetic words washed over me.

I was packed into the car, again. I was being driven home, again. Then I had my first food craving. I suppose that not only had the Guillain-Barré suppressed my appetite, but all those drugs may have also been to blame for my lack of food desire.

"Mom, I think I might be hungry," I whispered. What was this new sensation of hunger? I hadn't felt it in quite some time. "Actually, I think I'm craving food."

Starvation is an entirely different thing all together. I had been starving, and this was not that. This was craving; a deep desire for food. Actual hunger. I wanted to quench and satisfy that longing for the first time in months.

"You're hungry? What do you want? I'll get you anything." Excitement filled my mother's voice.

With as much relish as I could muster, I stated, "I want a...McDonald's cheeseburger!"

The most fattening and greasy thing to crave, and I suddenly wanted one. Immediately!

My mom was so excited she hung a sharp turn back to the nearest McDonald's. I thought she might get us into a car accident with the way she drove—as if our lives depended on us getting there quickly. And considering all, maybe that was true.

"Do you want two burgers? How about three? A milk-shake? Do you want fries too?" she rambled on.

"No, Mom, just one cheeseburger. I haven't eaten food in months and am not even sure I can eat this."

She whipped through that drive-through with a song on her lips and watched every single bite I slowly chewed and swallowed. She waited with a bowl just in case my stomach couldn't handle solid food. I ate the entire thing, and it stayed down. My stomach was working again! And I felt full.

A few days later, after eating and filling my belly, I was lying on the sofa and I began to hum. Music, joy, was flowing out of my mouth from deep inside my soul. I had continually had music inside of me during this dark journey, but I had been so weak that it stayed locked up inside my mind. Today, the music came out as a soft humming tune. Not much, but enough to catch my mother's attention. She heard me from the kitchen.

"Natalie, do you realize you are humming?"

"Well, no. Not out loud," I replied.

"You were humming out loud. Your joy is returning." My mom was jubilant. My joy must have been contagious because joy returned to my mother that day too.

I could see the light shining through my chrysalis. This cocoon had begun to crack.

TWENTY-SIX

DEBT-FREE, CAGE-FREE

A new commandment I give to you, that you love one another; as I have loved you, that you also love one another. By this all will know that you are My disciples, if you have love for one another.

JOHN 13:34-35
(NKJV)

One day, during my recovery, my mom received a phone call from the hospital's collections department. Due to the fact that we did not have medical insurance, my parents had already paid an exorbitant amount of money for all of the various bills, and more bills were rolling in.

"Mrs. Jeu, you owe XXX, XXX dollars," stated the caller.

"Okay, well, that is a lot of money and we don't have it right now, but can we get on some sort of payment plan?" queried my mom.

"Ma'am, is your daughter twenty?"

"Yes, she is."

"Well, technically, this debt is hers to pay. It is not yours and your husband's."

Pause.

Silence.

"Ma'am. Do you go to Faith West?" asked the caller.

"Yes, we go there," my mom answered.

"Well, your daughter is an inspiration. I have seen her go up and pray for others even though she was sick and dying. It brings tears to my eyes every time. Listen, this debt is hers, not yours. I know of some financial aid that I think she may qualify for. If you never hear from us again, consider the debt paid."

We never heard from another doctor or hospital again. Our bills were cleared, and I was now debt-free. No need to worry or walk in fear; God took care of it all.

The road to recovery was not easy. Yes, I knew I had been healed, but I still had to work out that healing journey, relearning everything I had done so easily before and piecing together the scraps of my external identity, watching to see if they would return to normal or be entirely different altogether.

At first, I played a lot of Connect 4—the small travel version. Therapist's orders. I had to practice "chipmunking," which is where you hold several of those tiny round game pieces in the palm of one hand, then, using only that one hand, slowly move a piece onto your fingertips and place it into the correct Connect 4 slot. I dropped a lot of game pieces. Over and over again, I would feel the small discs slip from my hand and hear them skitter along our glass breakfast tabletop. Ever so patiently, with much difficulty, I would then slowly pick each piece up again, with one hand, and begin chipmunking all over. Eventually, I was able to play the game right-handed or left-handed without dropping the pieces, putting them in the slots where I wanted them to go.

After I mastered chipmunking, I began coloring. Therapist's orders—again. I started with large coloring pages meant for toddlers and easy pictures with large spaces on them. I had to use crayons and try to stay inside the lines. For someone that hadn't truly held a writing utensil for weeks, I found this to be particularly difficult. The feel of the crayon was so foreign. It was heavy and lopsided in my fingers. I couldn't seem to apply enough pressure to hold it straight, so it kept leaning out from between my fingers and falling over. After much trial and error, I figured it out and I could color those kid pages. So I moved on to more detailed coloring pages and colored pencils.

Holding a pencil was so much more difficult than a crayon. It felt like my fingers hadn't learned anything at all. The pencils were longer and more slender and had a slippery quality to them, but over time I mastered coloring with them too.

Next, I was brave enough to try writing my name. I was so nervous. Could I do it? Would it even look like my handwriting? I had always prided myself on my small slanted script. I liked to make it pretty and I preferred to write in cursive. That day, I simply tried to print my name.

"I did it! It doesn't look very pretty though. Actually, it looks like a kindergartner trying to write their name for the first time," I stated. "But I think I can do this. Yes. I can do this. I will learn to write again. I will see my name in my own script again."

I also had begun trying to stand and walk on my own. Well, "walk" may be a bit dramatic. More like I would take a step to transition from my wheelchair to my bed or the sofa and then collapse into a semi-comfortable position. The important thing is that I was trying to do it myself, without any help.

My arms were so weak that lifting and steadying myself was like trying to use Jell-O as a support. I was wiggly and weak, and my movements were choppy at best. Good thing I still only weighed in the high seventies/low eighties range because my arms wouldn't have been able to support much more, even if it was only for a few seconds at a time. Speaking of arms, it was time to build their stamina too! So instead of letting everyone push me around in my wheelchair, I began rolling myself around. Over time I became an expert wheelchair driver.

My home, which I had so longed for during my hospital stays, became a bit of a cage as time ticked by. As my range of motion grew and I began to desire interaction with the world around me, I found myself wanting to get out of the house, even if only for a few moments at a time.

My mother and my boyfriend were extremely accommodating toward me and my whims. I would be sitting at home in my wheelchair and get the "itch" to go out. It wasn't like I could actually do much while I was out, but I just wanted to see, smell, and hear the world around me. Typically, I would ask to go to the mall. Katy Mills Mall was only a few miles away from us, so it was easy enough to go and come home without too much travel effort. Although there was still some effort involved.

"I need to get out of here, can we go to the mall?" I whispered to Wayne.

"Absolutely!" he declared with a huge smile on his face, as if he had just won the lottery instead of having to endure the task of taking his emaciated, wheelchair-bound, acne-faced girlfriend out in public.

Joyfully, he would wheel me out to his car, load me up, store the wheelchair in the trunk, then off we went. I was usually pretty tired just from the effort of getting in the car, but my desire to get out and about overrode my exhaustion.

Once at the mall, he would unload my wheelchair, get me comfortable, and then wheel me into the mall as fast as his long legs could walk. Wayne knew I never lasted long, so he would practically run inside. Once inside, he would push me around at top speed and pop wheelies for me in my chair. We laughed and enjoyed life just as we were.

Soon I would say, "I have to go home." My words were strained and weak from the exertion of the trip even though we had only been there a mere five to ten minutes.

"Okay," Wayne quipped, just as joyfully as if we had spent a full day out having fun.

Then he repeated the entire process in reverse until I was home safe, snuggled on the sofa watching a movie and falling asleep. This was a routine I repeated every few days with either him or my mom, and they never seemed to tire of accommodating all of my requests. They both had the patience of saints.

Today, it reminds me of the monotonous things my children ask me to do repetitively. As a mom I do have the grace to not only endure, but to enjoy and laugh in those moments. I remember the love extended to me when I was not able to do for myself and I try to reach down and pass that same love on to those around me.

TWENTY-SEVEN

WALKING

The faithful love of the Lord never ends! His mercies never cease.

LAMENTATIONS 3:22
(NLT)

I finally began to walk. Little steps at first. Simply moving from my wheelchair to another chair that was not right next to me. I needed a lot of help from another person, like my mom, when trying to travel "longer" distances only using my legs for support. It wasn't just my legs that were the problem, but my arms worked a bit like Jell-O. They weren't strong enough to push me up out of my chair and hold me up for more than a few seconds, and when I did finally manage to get up, they would tremble terribly until they collapsed. Several times this had me on my behind, or my face on the floor. I was determined that one day I would take those small steps from wheelchair to another chair on my own, without falling.

Once I regained better balance and strength, I then graduated to using an exceptionally fashionable walker. Nothing says sexy like an emaciated twenty-year-old woman using a silver granny walker with yellow cutout tennis balls on the bottom of the front two legs.

My dad returned that dreadful rented wheelchair the very same day I tried to use a walker at home for the first time. He didn't even ask me if I was done using it. He just loaded it up in his truck and returned home without it. I guess there was no going back at that point.

Although it never seemed to bother my family or boyfriend to be out in public with me and my "yellow Ferrari," I never did get very comfortable using it. I didn't care how wobbly I was using that thing, I couldn't build up my strength fast enough as beyond the walker came the next stage of glamour...a cane!

The cane stage lasted much longer than I wanted, but after losing all of my reflexes, muscle mass, and flexibility, I simply could not force myself to go without it. At least it was a brushed bronze color and did not have yellow tennis ball "upgrades." Actually, if I see someone using a cane incorrectly today, I have to suppress the urge to approach him or her, unsolicited, and teach them how to use it correctly. "Excuse me, Total Stranger, but did you know that you are using that cane incorrectly and throwing off your entire body's gait? You could cause long-lasting injury to your hips, spine, or knees! Here, let me, a fully able-bodied young whippersnapper, show you how to use it."

Good grief, I might get chased out of a grocery store by a little old lady and her cane.

After I left the cane behind, I simply held on to whoever was next to me for dear life! I usually went out with Wayne. I have no idea how he stuck around for so long, but he did. As we walked at a snail's pace wherever we went, he would either keep his arm around my waist or I would hold on to his elbow with a vise grip. I got tired easily, so frequent stops to sit and people-watch were always on the agenda.

One day we had the idea to go to the largest mall in our city, the Houston Galleria, which houses an ice-skating rink and three floors of shops; stairs, escalators, and elevators galore.

That was the day that I learned compassion. True compassion. Not that "Oh, I feel sorry for someone" or "I feel what you're going through" surface-level stuff but real, deep, heart-changing compassion. Plenty of people had been compassionate to my family and me along this journey, and I learned much from them about how to care for another going through crisis. They did it beautifully. But this compassion was something seen through the eyes of God.

Wayne and I were slowly making our way in and out of shops at the mall and found ourselves on the second level, looking over the glass railing to the shoppers on the ground below. I was hanging on to his elbow when a young lady approached me and tapped me on the shoulder.

"Yes?" I said, curious about what this young lady could want.

"You are absolutely beautiful," she breathed in a longing voice. Long pause. She gave me the once-over.

I wondered what she was thinking and sensed a hollowness inside of her. I wondered if she was going to say something sarcastic or rude to me, as some strangers who didn't know my medical history had been known to do, assuming that I was starving myself on purpose.

Instead she surprised me by saying, "I would give anything to be a skinny as you. You look amazing."

Compassion hit my heart like a sledgehammer. I took a good look at her and realized that she was either anorexic, bulimic, or both. Starving herself on purpose to look like me, a twenty-year-old Guillain-Barré survivor barely weighing in at ninety pounds and wearing size-zero clothes that were hanging off of me. I looked into her eyes, lifted my hand to her face, smiled my warmest and slightly wonky smile and said, "No, you wouldn't want to go through what I have gone through."

She looked at me a moment longer with a haunted stare. She then walked away with tears in her eyes and repeated, "Well, you look beautiful."

My heart ached! What has the world done to our girls? Our women? I was emaciated. I had truly been starved nearly to death. I was bones with flesh and clothes on. The spirit within me may have been beautiful, but the unhealthy, recovering-from-death survivor girl certainly was not. And no one should be starving themselves to reach that unrealistic goal of zero fat, zero muscle, and having their body shut down.

Starvation is cruel and loathsome. My heart cried for her. I wanted to sit and cry with her. I wanted to hug her and pour out the truth that her size did not equal her worth. I felt compassion through the heart of a seasoned survivor. I wanted the red-hot liquid love of Christ to pour into her and heal her from the inside out. But instead we parted ways.

I have often prayed for her to be released from the chains of lies that the enemy sold her, but I do not know what became of her.

Why pray? Because she is valued, she is worth much, she is loved.

My cocoon was splitting open with the light of day shining through and I was emerging, although weak with shriveled wings. But as I began to look around me, into the butterfly garden of life, now in my post-caterpillar and post-cocoon stage, I saw others that were still caterpillars, or many who were still trapped in their own chrysalises with the need to transform and break free. I saw these people and felt deep compassion. Some were ready for the transformation of life that was taking place as they allowed the Lord to guide them. Some were trapped in the darkness of their cocoons, ready to spend a lifetime there instead of allowing the pain of transformation and breaking free. They feared their wings and would rather stay inside their shell of darkness until death, instead of learning to fly.

Sometimes, what we view as our prison cell is actually a tool to be used in our future ministry toward others. Not that God places us in our prison or causes these terrible things to happen to us or around us. On the contrary—He uses the bad things brought on by our fallen world for good, in the end. It is like going to prison when wrongly accused, then being set free in the most miraculous way. That is how being placed inside a dark and silent cocoon might feel until the shell begins to crack open and the light of day filters in.

Looking back, my cocoon was Guillain-Barré and the loss of my independence. My chrysalis was illness, pain, paralysis, blindness, and the loss of those things that I thought made me, me. That is not the case for everyone. That tight, dark, lonely, yet brilliantly transformative, place can be any number of things. Examine your life. What ended your caterpillar eating days? When did circumstances begin spinning your cocoon?

Is your confining chamber **fear**?

Could **depression** be the web that has spun itself so tightly around you?

Are you **anxious**? **Lonely**? **Confused**?

What about your **body image**? Is it healthy, or do you see someone you don't like when you look in the mirror?

What words do you speak over yourself, inside your mind where no one else can hear? Does **worthlessness** reside inside your thoughts? Could that be the prison cell in which you dwell?

What words do you speak over others? Do you speak life or **death** into your family, your friends, and your children? Are you unintentionally building an early cocoon around the people in your life, around those you love?

Have you been **abused**? **Used**? **Mistreated**? **Misjudged**? **Misunderstood**?

What about **pride**? Could that be what imprisons you?

Does **addiction** hold you in its chains?

Have you been **abandoned**? **Unloved**? **Unwanted**?

Has **religion** let you down?

Does **something else** trap you where you are?

Do you think HELP! Set me FREE! There must be something else, something MORE?

Pause.

Stop.

Take a look back. When did it all start? How long have you been spinning your cocoon? How long have you let others spin it for you? How long have you been entangling those around you? How long have you been ensnared, hoping, waiting to be set free? Has it been too long? Is it time to start pushing out against those walls that hold you in their grip? Is it time for healing? For FREEDOM? For MORE?

Don't let those lessons you have learned inside your confining space go to waste. Don't let them die with you when you move from this life to the next. NO! Learn from them, heal through them—in spite of them—and break free so you can be a testimony to others.

God can use you for His glory.

The things we endure are to refine us, to make us radiant, and to give us wings to fly. Don't allow those "things," those circumstances, to beat you down and kill you. Cling to the One with answers. Cling to the One who has already set you free. His name is Jesus.

TWENTY-EIGHT

WINGS

*Long ago the Lord said to Israel: "I have loved you,
my people, with an everlasting love. With unfailing
love I have drawn you to myself.*

JEREMIAH 31:3

(NLT)

What is a butterfly?

It is beautiful. It flitters and flutters from flower to flower, seemingly never staying in one place very long. It is delicate and fragile. Short lived like a summer's breeze. Here today, then gone again after laying its eggs.

But NO! It is so much more than that.

Each butterfly is making generations of differences, sowing into the lives of every flower they touch. They pollinate and help new seeds form so the next generation of flowers has a chance to grow. It is their beautiful, delicate weakness—that flitty wandering—that makes them so very powerful. For if they sat in one place, never traveling and flying, they would never pollinate the beauty around them for the rest of us to enjoy. Much like us, if the butterfly simply stays in one place forever, multitudes of flowers would never be pollinated, and their next generations of seeds would never mature and grow.

Once we realize our worth and our calling, like the butterfly, we must not keep it locked up inside a cocoon. Rather, we must rise up, learn to fly, and go wherever He sends us! We are called to touch as many lives as the Lord leads us toward. We are called to pollinate those around us. To break chains, crack open cocoons, and help other caterpillars to become butterflies. To ensure the health of our future generations we must help those trapped caterpillars that are stuck in the tomb of a cocoon that was their old life. Help them overcome death and its dark sting and bring them into the victory of breaking free, into the tentative yet exciting new life that is set before them, if only they were to reach out and take it.

New beginnings start in a single moment. That moment turns into minutes, minutes into hours, hours into days, then weeks, months, and years. One day you look back and realize that your new beginning is not new anymore, it is your long journey from immediate freedom to a life of joy; the foundation of who you are today and who you are meant to become.

For me, time began to pass and my humanness began to come back. I could talk and walk and write. I was eating food and very slowly putting on weight. Those shriveled wings of mine began to fill out and show their magnificent beauty. Oh, what would I do with those new wings of mine?

Fly.

The flying part was both easy and difficult. I reached forward and grasped life at full force. I pushed further and tried harder. I didn't give up. The flying seemed to be the easier part; it was pollinating the flowers around me that took much more effort.

"Seven years," my doctor said. "It takes seven years for the body to heal from Guillain-Barré. Wherever your body is in seven years, it will remain for the rest of your life. No improvement past that point."

I thought on this and felt it was a good, long time to heal, but I also thought about all the things that might not be healed in seven years.

"Will I be able to drive again? Will I ever run or jump? Will my body be able to carry and bear children? Will the constant pain, tingling, arthritis, and strange sensations ever fully go away, or will they plague me for as long as I live?" Questions, so many questions and what-ifs. To ponder on them would drive a person crazy, so I laid them aside and moved forward moment by moment. Now, looking back, I simply wish I had relied on simple faith instead of doctor's reports, but I can't change my story, only learn from it.

There is a secret in living. It is enjoying the little things of life. The ordinary, the mundane. Not seeking out the next new and exciting moment that will exhilarate. Not being the adrenaline junkie or seeking out the next wave of joy that will be like riding a high. No. Life IS the high. And Jesus is the reason we get to enjoy it...all of it. The tough times mold us, the grueling moments shape us, the isolation transforms us. When all we can do is lean on the Lord, He can take over and fashion new and beautiful wings for us that will allow us to do something we never even imagined was possible: lift up on the whisper of a breeze and fly.

"Let me take you out on a date?" my boyfriend queried. "This weekend we will get all dressed up and I will take you to dinner at a fancy restaurant." It was now March 2001. I had been on this journey for about ten months.

"Okay. That sounds like fun." Actually, it sounded magnificent. A "real date" where we get all dressed up and go out like a real couple that has not been fighting a long and arduous battle.

That weekend Wayne came knocking on my door wearing a suit, and I was all dressed up in the prettiest thing I could find that would still fit my diminished frame. With makeup on and my hair styled, I climbed into his car and we went off to eat Italian in town at Carmello's. My spirits were so lifted I felt like I was walking on air instead of hanging on to his arm for dear life.

Unfortunately, Wayne had suddenly come down with a horrible case of seasonal allergies and was feeling dreadful, but he didn't have it in him to postpone the date I had been so looking forward to. We arrived early to miss much of the dinner crowd and yet we were somehow seated at a table placed next to the loudest bunch of diners. I can only assume they were there celebrating due to their great revelry, animated gestures, and booming voices.

I tried to sit and enjoy my food, and this time away on a date, but I could see that Wayne was having difficulty relaxing. He was feeling yucky with the allergies and was restless. He gobbled his food down at warp speed and wanted to leave as soon as possible. I wasn't quite ready to leave but acquiesced to his request.

With my leftover food to-go box in hand, we drove over to a small lake and decided to take a romantic stroll hand in hand (really, it was my hand in the crook of Wayne's arm so I wouldn't fall). It was getting dark outside when Wayne stopped me under a light near the pond and knelt down on one knee. With a tissue held up to his dripping nose, he plunged forward into a proposal. "Natalie, I'm sorry I have allergies and don't feel great, but I can't wait any longer. Will you marry me?"

After all we had been through. While still battling and surrounded by questions of my future, here he was proclaiming his love for me and his willingness to stand by me in life, come what may. He had stuck by me through thick and thin thus far and he wanted to stick by me forevermore.

"Yes!"

We were engaged!

We would get married the following March. I spent the next year of our engagement preparing for our wedding, getting my fiancé graduated from college and his new career started, strengthening my body enough to walk down the aisle in a white dress without falling over, and so much more.

I started working as a bank teller, which was good for me. I worked close to home and could sit down whenever my body was tired. I was also still drinking that hyped-up energy drink to make it through the days. I was finally able to start driving again and interacting with people daily at the bank brought me back to the "real" world. Also, earning and saving money for our new life to come was an accomplishment that I hadn't been sure I would ever get to have when I was lying in the hospital, but here I was doing just that.

On a spur-of-the-moment outing, Wayne and I went back to the Galleria mall we had gone to when I had been barely recovering. The same place where we met that hurting young woman intent on being skinny. This time we were approached by another stranger, a young man no less. This young man walked up to us, looked me right in the eye and said, "You two will have beautiful children." He flashed a sparkling smile and walked away. I wasn't even sure if I could have children after my health ordeal, but his words struck a chord deep inside me as if I had just been prophesied over.

The year seemed to both crawl and fly by, and before I knew it the big day had come! Although pain was my constant companion, joy was also my constant helper. The day of preparation with my family, friends, and soon-to-be new sisters was exciting and perfect. I would not change a single detail of our magical wedding day where all those that had walked through this difficult journey with us surrounded me!

Once ready and at the church, I could hear the string quartet playing as my bridesmaids walked down the aisle. I held my dad's arm, waiting patiently for my turn to go. He stopped me for one moment and said, "You sure you want to do this? I have my truck outside; we can still run. You are not married until you say, 'I do.'"

I smiled, giggled and said, "Yes, I'm sure, Daddy. I'm not going to run."

That may seem silly but, looking back, that is one of my favorite things about my dad. He always gave me an out. In any situation, good or bad, he made sure that I was doing what I should be doing no matter the cost. He had my back and would readily help me "run," even after paying for all of the wedding costs, if I had any doubt that I shouldn't be where I was.

I didn't run, but I did walk down the aisle. I walked toward a future that during my illness I wasn't sure I would ever have the privilege of living. I walked toward the unknown and knew that, just like my daddy, God had my back, whatever may come.

After exchanging our vows, we had a time of communion and worship, and the most spectacular thing happened. Our wedding photographer had arrived at our wedding in tremendous pain. Apparently, her back had been hurting her for quite some time and was getting worse. She was a little worried about getting through the entire evening but trudged on with a brave face anyway. During the time of worship, the photographer said she suddenly felt warmth spread through her body and wrap around her back. Instantly she was healed. All her pain was gone and she finished off the night taking pictures with a joyful spring in her step. God honored us by using our wedding as a time of physical healing for someone else!

TWENTY-NINE

FULLY HEALED

Yours, O Lord, is the greatness, the power and the glory, the victory and the majesty; for all that is in Heaven and in Earth is Yours; Yours is the kingdom, O Lord, and You are exalted as head over all. Both riches and honor come from You, and You reign over all. In Your hand is power and might; in Your hand it is to make great and to give strength to all.

I CHRONICLES 29:11-12
(NKJV)

After our enchanting wedding day, Wayne and I enjoyed time on our honeymoon, then came back home to our new apartment and jobs. Life went on as I would imagine many newlyweds' lives start out, except for a few things. One, I was in constant pain. Even though I now looked "normal"—just a bit skinny to the onlooker—and even though I worked full-time and lived the life of a wife, cooking, cleaning, and grocery shopping, my body was still inflicted by the residual effects from Guillain-Barré. The acne that had plagued me during my illness was gone, and the clumps of hair I had lost had grown back. I had gained weight and was now in the low ninety pounds. I wore tiny double zero clothes but my stamina was strong. Getting through the day with energy was no longer too difficult, so I had completely stopped drinking energy drinks. I also had my balance and most of my reflexes back!

But the pain was relentless. My hands and feet tingled with neuropathy pain continually, and my face would tingle when I was stressed or overburdened. The right side of my face was still slightly paralyzed and I struggled with restless leg syndrome at night when trying to fall asleep. Not only that, but the arthritis in my hips was unyielding! Climbing the stairs in our cute two-story loft apartment was torturous. I often wouldn't even go upstairs until my husband came home so he could carry me up. The arthritis was especially heightened when it rained. What is it about rain and pain? Those nights I would usually end up sleeping on the sofa downstairs instead of venturing up and down with hubby's help.

Second, I had no idea if we could have kids. We simply assumed we would be able to when we were ready, but the question of conception and then birth was a big one in the back of my mind. After being paralyzed it was hard to know what was fully functioning as time went on, but God knew.

Third, we decided to not have a television during the first year of our marriage. This is something I highly recommend to all newly married couples. I don't remember if we made the decision purposefully or if we just wanted to save money by not spending it on non-necessary expenses, but it turned out to be a great asset. No television distractions required us to spend time together and to talk face-to-face instead of "checking out" into the pixelated world of fantasy. I feel like this bonded and strengthened us as a couple.

While living in our little loft apartment, we began to build our first home. We called it our "starter home" and had "plans." Sometimes I think God laughs when we make plans of our own. Not in a mocking way but in a joyful "wait until you see what I have for you" way. His ways are, after all, good and perfect.

We moved into our "starter home" a few weeks before our first anniversary. Our "plan" was to have our first and maybe second child there, then move to a larger house with a real backyard. We would have kids three years after getting married, have one or two children, then move and blah, blah, blah. Ha!

For us marriage was wonderful, easy, hard, and challenging all at once. We loved each other deeply, and my relationship with the Lord was constantly growing. Just like all newlywed couples, we agreed, disagreed, fought together, and laughed together. In both the difficult and easy times, I found myself leaning on the Lord for my strength because no matter how amazing my husband was, and is, he was not the answer to it all. God was and is the answer.

After a while in our new home and new church, I felt like God was calling me to more. He had given me much in my life and now it was time for me to begin giving back; for me to begin not only flying but also pollinating those around me. So I asked Him where He wanted me, and He answered. Ever since I was a little girl, I had felt like God told me I would have or be in a healing ministry one day. Oh sure, I had prayed for people throughout my life and had seen many healed miraculously before me, some healed over time, and some even dying.

I wouldn't call that a healing ministry but rather a prayer ministry. Prayer...what a beautiful thing. Prayer is powerful, and when lined up with the will of God, it never comes back void. I also believe that it IS God's will for everyone to be healed. After all, Jesus already paid the price for everyone's complete healing through the stripes He bore, and when asked, He healed ALL that came to Him. As to why we don't always see that happen, that would be an entirely other book of its own, but I do know that God is still The Healer, and it IS His will for all of you to be healed today!

I also firmly believe that although God did not give me Guillain-Barré, He was and still is using it in the healing ministry that He has for me. I was touched by blindness, pain, arthritis, neuropathy, isolation, paralysis, loss, and so much more. Not only living through those things and surviving them, thriving beyond them has given me a compassion for others that I would probably not have had without the experience. Now I understand others' pain. Now I remember the darkness of being blind. Now I have compassion for desperation and loneliness.

God has always spoken to me in whispers, dreams, visions, through His words and through others. When I asked Him where He wanted me to minister, He directed me to the healing ministry at our church. So even though I still struggled with pain of my own, I joined up and began laying hands on others to see them healed. Many, many were miraculously healed in front of my eyes and others came back to share their healing testimonies with me at a later date.

While serving in this ministry of healing, the most marvelous and miraculous thing happened. Wayne and I found ourselves expecting our first child after five years of marriage and immediately upon trying to have a baby. Actually, our first daughter was born just a few weeks before our sixth wedding anniversary. And this is where the hand of the sovereign Lord fell upon us and completed the work He had begun.

I conceived our daughter, and immediately upon becoming pregnant, the REST of my healing was completed. Every last bit. Just a few weeks past conception, I woke up one morning realizing that everything had changed in an instant. The pain and arthritis left. The micro paralysis in many of my muscles was gone. The painful tingling in my hands, feet, and face vanished. Not only that, before I had been ill, I wore glasses and contacts and now my vision was 20/10. The seasonal allergies I once suffered disappeared. The regular headaches I endured never returned. God went above and beyond the call of healing Guillain-Barré duty and healed exceedingly more than I could have asked or hoped for.

Through the loving conception of my daughter, the complete manifestation of God's miraculous healing was finished. The healing that had started years before when my pastor prayed his most simple and vulnerable prayer, which collided with all the prayers that had gone before and come after. Our God is timeless! I WAS HEALED and I was flying free! I was finally a butterfly!

All of my doctors agreed that they never wanted to see me in a hospital again, so their blessings were given for me to use my preferred method for prenatal care and birth: a midwife and homebirth! It was a joyous and marvelous journey carrying a tiny life inside of me while my body and energy were perfected. I was on the healing team at our church AND I was healed! What a blissful and faith-building testimony to share with those I would pray with from that day forward.

In John 14:12-14 (NKJV) Jesus says, "Most assuredly, I say to you, he who believes in Me, those works that I do he will do also; and greater works than these he will do, because I go to My Father. And whatever you ask in My name, that I will do, that the Father may be glorified in the Son. If you ask anything in My name, I will do it."

THIRTY

MORE

But he who prophesies speaks edification and exhortation and comfort to men.

I CORINTHIANS 14:3
(NKJV)

We can allow the circumstances we go through in life to do a number of things to us. We can become bitter, asking questions like, "Why me?" or "How can a loving God do this to me?" Or we can rise above the situation and let it refine us. Bringing us into a place of dependency and intimacy with the loving God that did not cause these things to happen to us, but rather is able to use the "bad things" in our lives and turn them into good.

In her younger years, a caterpillar's body must get fat, much like our faith should be growing in order to survive the refining that life brings along. She lives on that fat in her lonely, dark cocoon to be made new, to grow wings. When she emerges, her body is much leaner and her new wings are wet and wrinkled. She looks different, she feels different, but her mind remains the same. She is still herself, but altogether something new. She begins to recover and her wings fill, becoming rigid and strong. Soon, very soon, they will lift her off the ground of her old, fat-building life and she will fly! To experience the weightlessness and freedom that was to become hers, from God.

My husband and I went on to have two more children—also homebirths with our midwife. I joined the prayer altar team and the prophetic prayer ministries at our church, which are magnificently fulfilling and glorious.

Since then, our sweet family of five has moved to the "half-country" as I jokingly call it, since we are still very near major cities, and joined a much smaller church near our new home. We continue our daily lives of homeschooling, partnering up in prayer ministries, raising our chickens, gardening, and hopefully listening to and obeying God. He still speaks to me regularly through dreams, visions, and in the prophetic, but I expect that He has even more headed our way.

Although my views on healing have strengthened and changed over the years, this book is the story of how it took place in my life. I believe you don't have to have, or should have, a long journey of healing but rather that God can, and will, reach down and touch you this very moment. He is such a gentleman and works with us right where we are.

I no longer think of my life in terms of pre-Guillain-Barré or post-Guillain-Barré. Too much wonderful life has taken place since, so now I just live in the moment of what is placed before me.

God moves us and changes our lives depending on different seasons. We may stay in one place for a long time, or even forever, or we may be moved to new and strange things, but with God on our side, we can step out in faith and follow Him. Through our trials and pain, He is sculpting and creating something beautiful and new. He is making you into a butterfly too.

THE END

PICTURES

20th Surprise Birthday August 2000

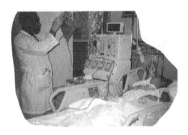

Plasmapheresis 2000

Homemade Cookies Gift

Drying Flower Seeds

Engaged May 2001

Right side of face still paralyzed

Just Married March 2002

Fully Healed 37 weeks pregnant 2008

Natalie Today, December 2020

Who is this man Jesus?

If we took a survey asking people around the world, "Who is Jesus?" we would receive many different answers. Some would say "He was a Jewish carpenter, the son of Mary," others may respond "He was a good man." Another response may pronounce Jesus as a "holy man," a "teacher," or even a "prophet of God." And although Jesus may be all of those things, he is also so much more.

Jesus' Identity According to the Bible

For those of you that do not know Jesus as your personal Lord and Savior, or maybe have never even heard the name of Jesus before reading this book, we need to dig a little deeper.

In *Isaiah 60:1-2* we learn that God "is a good Father" and that He is "for you and not against you." Sometimes it feels like if there is a God, He must be against you on every front, and you blame Him for all the things going wrong in your life. According to the Word of God, that is not true. God is

FOR YOU! There is an enemy too, and he (that enemy Satan) is the one that is against you, but let's not jump ahead, we will get back to the enemy in a moment.

John 3:16-17 (*NKJV*) says, "For God so loved the world that He gave His only begotten Son, that whoever believes in Him should not perish but have everlasting life. For God did not send His Son into the world to condemn the world, but that the world through Him might be saved." We learn here that Jesus is God's son, and that God gave us His only Son, Jesus, as a gift.

The Apostle Paul further describes who Jesus is in *Colossians* 1:15-17 (*NKJV*) "The Son is the image of the invisible God, the firstborn over all creation. For in him all things were created: things in heaven and on earth, visible and invisible, whether thrones or powers or rulers or authorities; all things have been created through him and for him. He is before all things, and in him all things hold together." Wow! What a beautiful and powerful description of Jesus. He is the creator of all things and holds all things together.

And *John* 10:10 reveals to us that Jesus came to give us life. Why do we need life from Jesus?

Why did Jesus come to give life? Because God has an enemy!

Yes, God has an enemy and his name is Satan. Satan is not some fictional cartoon character, rather he is very real. *John* 10:10 (*NKJV*) "The thief does not come except to steal, and to kill, and to destroy. I have come that they may have life, and that they may have it more abundantly." Satan brought sin into the world through Eve's temptation to rebel against God. You can read the full account of man's fall through sin in Genesis chapter 3. And according to *Romans 6:23a* (*NIV*), "For the wages of sin is death." That is the bad news. ALL mankind are born with the nature of the fallen sinful man, meaning we ALL sin. So, exactly what is sin? Sin is an archery term that literally means to "miss the mark." Sin is missing the mark of God's perfection. Or, not being 100% perfect 100% of the time, or missing the bull's-eye. I don't know a single person that has never missed the mark or not messed up somewhere in life at some point in time! Do you? Hmm, so that means every single human being, that's all of us, fall into the "sinner" category. *Romans 6:23a*, tells us the wage (or price) for sin is death. That means we all deserve the penalty of death because all of us have sinned and fall short of perfection.

Great news!

"But God demonstrates His own love toward us, in that while we were still sinners, Christ died for us. Much more then, having now been justified by His blood, we shall be saved from wrath through Him." *Romans 5:8-9* (*NKJV*)

Jesus' coming was foretold in the Old Testament Scriptures.

Isaiah 53:4-9 (*NKJV*) prophesies these words: "Surely He has borne our griefs and carried our sorrows; yet we esteemed Him stricken, smitten by God, and afflicted. But He was wounded for our transgressions, He was bruised for our iniquities, the chastisement for our peace was upon Him, and by His stripes we are healed. All we like sheep have gone astray; we have turned, everyone, to his own way, and the Lord has laid on Him the iniquity of us all. He was oppressed and He was afflicted, yet He opened not His mouth. He was led as a lamb to the slaughter, and as a sheep before its shearers is silent, so He opened not His mouth. He was taken from prison and from judgment, and who will declare His generation? For He was cut off from the land of the living; for the transgressions of My people He was stricken. And they made His grave with the wicked—but with the rich at His death, because He had done no violence, nor was any deceit in His mouth."

The gift of God is Jesus and eternal life.

John 3:16-17 (*NKJV*) says, "For God so loved the world that He gave His only begotten Son, that whoever believes in Him should not perish but have everlasting life. For God did not send His Son into the world to condemn the world, but that the world through Him might be saved."

Jesus is the gift that was given for us and to us. He paid the penalty of sin and death so we would not have to die eternally. He was accused of blasphemy; He was whipped, beaten, and bruised for our illnesses and diseases. He was sent by his own people to die a bloody and gruesome death on a Roman cross where He, Jesus, the God/man, would then carry the sins of the entire world upon Himself.

He that knew NO SIN became sin, for us.

He did it willingly, without arguing or saying a word.

Why? Because He wanted to pay for the sins that WE had committed but could not meet the expense of. He did not fight against his torture and sacrifice; rather He poured Himself out for us. One drop of His perfect blood would have been enough, but HE POURED HIMSELF OUT for

US! He gave all! With His blood spilled, the gruesomeness of death and sin was then carried to the grave on our behalf.

Jesus' power over death, Hell, and the grave... what does it mean?

Down in the grave where death and Hell reside, Jesus dragged down and buried the sins of the world and defeated the author of those sins, Satan. In *Revelation 1:18* (*NKJV*) Jesus declares, "I am He who lives, and was dead, and behold, I am alive forevermore. Amen. And I have the keys of Hades and of Death."

Jesus took back that power we lost to Satan. The keys we handed over to the devil when sin entered the world. Jesus took them back and now holds them and offers Himself as deliverer. After three days and nights in the grave, Jesus rose again. He is alive today. He holds the keys to Hell, death, and the grave. He holds that power; it is no longer Satan's. All we have to do to be released from the prison of sin is to ask. There is nothing we can do on our own to save ourselves; it is 100% through grace and acceptance of Jesus Christ as our Lord and Savior.

Titus 3:4-7 (*NKJV*) says, "But when the kindness and the love of God our Savior toward man appeared, not by works of righteousness which we have done, but according to His mercy. He saved us, through the washing of regeneration and renewing of the Holy Spirit, whom He poured out on us abundantly through Jesus Christ our Savior, that having been justified by His grace we should become heirs according to the hope of eternal life."

Satan is the tempter, the accuser, and the destroyer. Satan deserves the blame we so often place on God. It is Jesus that defeated this enemy along with death, Hell, and the grave. Jesus defeated ALL sin when He died on the cross, then He rose again from the dead three days after His crucifixion. Jesus is ALIVE today and is ready to give you a seat at His banquet table. The invitation is extended, your seat is reserved, will you come? Will you sit? Will you eat of the food of life that the Lord has set before you? If so, then accept Him right now.

There are only two options in this world: Heaven vs. Hell or also stated Jesus vs. Satan, and if you do not intentionally choose Heaven and Jesus, then by default you will have chosen Hell and Satan. "Today I have given you the choice between life and death, between blessings and curses. Now I call on Heaven and Earth to witness the choice you make. Oh, that you would choose life, so that you and your descendants might live!" *Deuteronomy* 30:19 (*NLT*) Choose Life!

No one wants to die! Eternity is written in our hearts.

All of us would love it if death was abolished and we could live forever. Scripture tells us that eternity is in our hearts. No one wants to die!

According to the second half of *Romans* 6:23 (*NIV, emphasis added*), "For the wages of sin is death, but **the gift of God is eternal life in Christ Jesus our Lord**," we can have that eternal life we so desire.

How do we get this gift of eternal life? How do we make Jesus our Lord? How do we receive Jesus and eternal life? You choose to believe there is a gift, then receive the gift when offered.

The gift is Jesus and you receive Him by **believing** what God tells us about His Son. Then once you believe, you **repent** of your sins. Repent means to acknowledge you are a sinner in need of a Savior and turning away from a life of sin. Then **ask** God's Son to save you by allowing Jesus to be the Lord of your life.

Know and understand these 3 things: **One**: (*I John 5:13*) You will be saved spiritually and gain eternal life. **Two**: (*James 5:14*) You will be saved physically, and all manner of healing will belong to you immediately. **Three**: You will be saved mentally so that all sinful thoughts, lusts, temptations, and chaos of the mind can be instantly corrected and healed. You can have a sound mind today. Remember, it is all about your Faith in Christ, believing the Father's words about His Son; it's about your intentions and surrender of the heart before a holy and loving God.

Pray out loud to Father God in the name of His Son, Jesus, and realize the surrender that is set before you.

"Jesus, I realize now that I am a sinner. I know that because of my sin, I cannot stand before a Holy God and that I am doomed to death, Hell, and the grave apart from Christ.

Jesus, your death has made a way for me to know the Father God. Because you have shed your blood for me, my sins can be washed away.

Jesus, I receive you today and I ask you to forgive me of my sins. I choose to turn from my old life and turn to you now thru repentance of all my sins and any way that displeases you. Forgive me for my transgressions and cleanse me white as snow with your blood that you shed on the cross for me. Renew my mind thru your Word and heal my body for your word says I am healed by the stripes You bore on your back for me.

I accept Your invitation for salvation. Come into my life and be my Lord and my Savior. Transform me into the person You created me to be.

I love You, Jesus! Now help me to love others and myself, and to follow You all the days of my life. Reveal Your perfect plan for my life to me and help me to walk it out in joyful and faithful abandon as I remain consecrated to You. In Your Mighty Name I Pray, Jesus. Amen."

Who the Bible says you are in Christ.

The Bible says that once you accept Jesus as your Lord and Savior, you are an ambassador of Christ (*II Corinthians* 5:20). You are already seated in the heavenly places (*Ephesians* 2:6). You are the temple of the Holy Spirit (*I Corinthians* 3:16-17, *I Corinthians* 6:19-20). As such you have the power and authority to speak, declare, and proclaim the will of God over your life, and to have the faith to fully accept that perfect will of God (*Romans* 12:12). That includes speaking and declaring healing over yourself and others. After all, Jesus commanded us, "As you go, preach, saying, 'The kingdom of Heaven is at hand.' Heal the sick, cleanse the lepers, raise the dead, cast out demons.

Freely you have received, freely give." (*Matthew* 10:7-8 *NKJV*)

Jesus is the Chain Breaker. He is the Freedom Maker. He is the Healer, Jehovah Raphe; the One that makes all things NEW. Jesus is God come in the flesh that lived, died, rose again, and is still ALIVE today. Jesus—He LOVES you!

2 Corinthians 5:17 (*NKJV*) says, "Therefore, if anyone is in Christ, he is a new creation; old things have passed away, behold, all things have become new."

Now go tell someone and get into a Bible teaching church! **Declare** Jesus as Lord for all to hear, and show your example to others by being water baptized. Never stop learning about Jesus by reading the Word of God (the Bible).

APPENDIX B

HEALING PRAYER

I believe that God still heals today, and that the gifts of the Spirit have not passed away but are in full force working in tandem with the Lord's will as we seek our relationship with Him. Jesus actually commands us to go "Heal the Sick" in the Bible because He has already paid the price at the scourging post and appointed us as His ambassadors! First, you need to repent and ask Jesus to be your Lord and Savior (see Appendix A). The word of God says, "Beloved, I wish above all things that thou mayest prosper and be in health, even as thy soul prospereth." *3 John 1:2 (KJV)*

It is His desire to see everyone saved, delivered, healed, and set free. The Greek word for Salvation that is used in the New Testament of the Bible is "sozo." According to Biblestudytools.com, the definition of sozo is to save, keep safe and sound, to rescue from danger or destruction; to save a suffering one from perishing; **to save one suffering from disease, to make well, heal, restore to health**; to save or rescue (as from sin and Hell). So, technically, Biblical Salvation is for the **spirit** (to go to Heaven), the **soul** (to have a sound mind and emotions), and the **body** (physical healing). So let us pray the following prayer of faith together knowing it is God's will to sozo (save) you in all areas.

"Dear Heavenly Father,

Thank You for the friends You have reading this book. I know You brought them here for a purpose and a reason that we may not realize right now, but that You are working all things together for good.

"Jesus, I thank You that You are the healer, Jehovah Rophe. I thank You that You hear my cries for help. You love me and you care deeply. I thank You that You have never left me, and that I can enter boldly into Your throne room and make my requests known. Jesus, I call on Your name now. I claim the pain You bore and the blood You shed for me. Through this book the Kingdom of Heaven has come near me today, and by the stripes Jesus bore; I AM HEALED! Thank You for touching my body, my mind, and my heart. Thank You for restoring my finances, my relationships, and my emotions. Thank You that I am healed completely from the inside out. I ask that you place Your hand upon me so that the enemy of my soul is unable to move in my life. Hide me under the shadow of Your wings. I love You. By Jesus' stripes I am healed.

Thank You! In Jesus' name I pray. Amen."

APPENDIX C

LIFESTYLE FOR HEALTH & HEALING

For me, the number one help for living a life of health and healing is Jesus. The Bible says, "Beloved, I wish above all things that thou mayest prosper and be in health, even as thy soul prospereth." *3 John 1:2 (KJV)* So it stands to reason that our bodies will often echo our soul in health. Another great asset, apart from your personal walk with the Lord, is a healing ministry, or a fellow Christ follower with the gift of faith and healing that is walking in the power of the Holy Spirit. Call on those to anoint you with oil and pray over you.

There are several social media support groups for Guillain-Barré syndrome and other such devastating illnesses, so if you or someone you know is suffering, don't go through it alone. Reach out, ask for help, keep pushing for answers, and seek out that person who is able and willing to lay hands on you and command your healing.

I discovered that pure, therapeutic-grade essential oils really helped me toward the end of my recovery. I didn't discover

Young Living Essential Oils until just before my pregnancy with my first child. At that time, I still struggled with severe arthritis pain, tingling neuropathy pain, paralysis, low energy, and restless legs. For me, personally, a few different Young Living oils, such as lavender, Peace and Calming, cypress, and frankincense, diluted and applied directly to the area of need, helped soothe my body enough for me to go to sleep at night and get a good rest. I also enjoyed drinking NingXia Red daily to help boost my energy and aid in daily bodily needs.

After my personal experience with vaccinations, illness, and hospitals, my doctors never wanted to see me seriously ill or in a hospital again. I began down a very natural path of prayer, organic foods, exercise, all-natural products, and healthy living wherever possible. Along with that, I use natural aids, such as essential oils, and drink superfood green juices and smoothies, which help both my family and me stay on a path of health. If you are looking to purchase oils, feel free to do so under me—Natalie Sherwood - YL Distributor #: 1069772 @ youngliving.com

ABOUT THE AUTHOR

Natalie Sherwood came to the saving knowledge of Jesus Christ at the age of six and has been on the ride of her life ever since. As a little girl she would often remark, "Why do I have to learn this English grammar stuff? It's not like God is ever going to make me write a book!" God sure does have a sense of humor.

Natalie is a native Texan whose favorite word is *y'all*. She has been part of multiple prayer ministries including Prayer Altar, Healing Prayer, Prophetic Prayer, Freedom and Healing, and Spiritual Housecleaning ministries, but her favorite prayer time is when she communes with the Lord all day long during her normal everyday tasks. It is Natalie's greatest pleasure to watch people in her path be completely healed and set free through Christ; after all, eternity begins now.

Natalie enjoys gardening, reading, prophetic pour painting, and the great outdoors. She currently lives in the grand state of Texas with her husband, Wayne, her three children, Mackenzie, Micah, and Selah, a bunny rabbit named Shofar, and a handful of chickens.

To contact Natalie, please send emails to: hisredemptionroad@gmail.com

Printed in Great Britain
by Amazon